COMMUNITY
PSYCHOLOGY AND
COORDINATION

COMMUNICATION SCIENCE
AND TECHNOLOGY

Designed for Communication Leaders in the Media, Libraries and Information Specialization

PATRICK R. PENLAND, *Editor*

1. Communication Science and Technology, *Patrick R. Penland*
2. Interpersonal Communication, *Patrick R. Penland & Aleyamma Mathai*
3. Group Dynamics and Personal Development, *Patrick R. Penland & Sara Fine*
4. Community Psychology and Coordination, *Patrick R. Penland & Jim Williams*
5. Nonverbal Communication, *Ellen McCardle*

Volumes in Preparation

6. Simulation Games, *James G. Williams & Elspeth Pope*

COMMUNITY PSYCHOLOGY AND COORDINATION

Patrick R. Penland
UNIVERSITY OF PITTSBURGH
PITTSBURGH, PENNSYLVANIA

James G. Williams
UNIVERSITY OF SOUTH CAROLINA
COLUMBIA, SOUTH CAROLINA

MARCEL DEKKER, INC. New York 1974

MARCEL DEKKER, INC.

270 Madison Avenue, New York, New York 10016

LIBRARY OF CONGRESS CATALOG CARD NUMBER: 74-77111

ISBN: 0-8247-6144-8

Current printing (last digit):
10 9 8 7 6 5 4 3 2 1

PRINTED IN THE UNITED STATES OF AMERICA

COMMUNICATION SCIENCE AND TECHNOLOGY

An Introduction to the Series

Since midcentury there has been an exponential increase in the volume of recorded knowledge and a revolution in the control and transfer of information by means of electronic technology. These changes have not only brought the resource specializations of media, library, and information science into a closer working relationship, but have been the impetus for the creation of a new profession, that of resource communicator. Resource sharing and computer networking have made it difficult for these three specializations to hang onto outmoded autonomies. Creative professionals have been released by technology to explore their role as advocates and agents of change in the affairs of human beings. This commonality of concern for people, as distinct from the production, control, and transfer of materials, is slowly being articulated by leaders in the three specializations.

The common profession of communicator, whose objective is to develop communication services based on a network of all-encompassing resource infrastructures, has emerged from the specializations of media, library, and information science. In practice, of course, some variations may still exist in the services provided. With this series these variations need no longer receive greater attention than the needs of the whole human being seeking help for his own behavioral self-control and self-design. As a result, the client need no longer be shunted around from media center to library and adult-education agency or to information center regardless of the fact that it is the surprise value of knowledge within a behavioral context which he needs and not necessarily the documents and resources guarded by each type of resource agency.

The general purpose of publications in the Communication Science and Technology series is to integrate professional and historical developments, as so many other texts in the field do not. These publications feature a service-oriented and conceptually-interlocking system of communication principles and communication services based within the traditions and practice of media, libraries, and information science. Publications in the series provide the basis for a bold new approach for the resource communicator, one which emphasizes communication over agency standards, deals directly with the problems of living rather than with documentation, and meets controversy when and where it arises in the neighborhood without traveling to the media, library, or information center.

The disciplines that create new knowledge will be interested in this approach to the development of communications. The profession of resource communicator holds considerable promise as a significant social method for more rapidly closing the gap between research findings and their application to the affairs of the common man. In addition, the series will be of singular importance to any profession which employs the resources of recorded knowledge to solve human problems or develops guidelines for planned social change, such as is done in education, communications, and politics. A case in point is adult education, the principles and methods of which have long served as a source of inspiration and guidance to librarians. These professions can view the emergence of resource communicators not as an encroachment upon their affairs but as an opportunity for enhanced partnership in serving public needs.

These publications can be employed as guides for practice, in-service training, and the continuing education of resource-center staff. The theoretical foundations of behavioral psychology, group-systems analysis, and community sociodrama will be of particular significance to the busy supervisor called upon to provide a rationale for communication services in media, libraries, and information centers. Within this framework the methods and techniques are developed for creating, channeling, and applying information surprise to the concerns and interests of the patron whether as an individual, a small group, or the neighborhood and community enterprise.

These publications will help the profession to create the conditions within which communicative activity can occur. Through communication, it will enhance its image as a socially accountable profession which can handle socially unstable subsystems. More specifically, the reader, be he general or professional, will find answers to questions such as the following.

What social purposes, function, and even, procedures do the resource professions share with each other and with other professions in society?

> For what social change among which publics are the resource professions responsible? Within what contexts can the change process be carried out by resource communicators?

> What means can be employed to accomplish planned social change? What factors can be exploited in order to motivate citizens to participate and to communicate?

> How can the infrastructure of resources be deployed in order to support a communications profession? How can the gap between indexed message space and the nonverbal and audio-visual message space of the people be closed?

The volumes in the series may be used as textbooks, supplementary readings, or as background reading for the informed citizen, especially the wide range of persons who use media, libraries, and information centers as well as those who serve as trustees or board members of institutions which maintain resource centers. The volumes in the series cover concepts and describe methods that would be useful in particular for

> Audiovisual and media specialists in a wide range of centers serving patrons with various socioeconomic, cultural, and educational levels

> Librarians in all types of agencies and who provide services to patrons of varying age levels, education, and socioeconomic status

> Information specialists, including systems analysts and designers, at various levels of service

> The broad range of adult education facilities administered by a variety of institutions and agencies as well as educators at all levels and, in particular, media and library and information science faculties

> Sociologists, political scientists and politicians, urbanologists and urban information systems specialists

> Community planners (urban planners), public administrators, community leaders (lay and professional), communication specialists (all levels)

Professional staff and lay volunteers of the numerous
information hot lines and neighborhood information
centers

The models presented and the methods discussed are fundamental
to human affective and cognitive development as it is achieved through
communicative processes. The professional concerned about his own
self-development may wish to peruse these publications for insight into
what is known about human intellectual growth and development. As a
result he may be able to remain in control of his own growth, independent
of outside influences. On the other hand, in those instances when he
finds it useful to seek help from other communicators, the professional
role will become more meaningful and productive for him.

Since the meaning of communication is not self-evident, the resource
professions need a definition and explication of a communicative profession and the relation of applications to the contexts of dyad, group,
and community. With a formulated behavior theory integrated with the
principles of media, library and information science it should be possible
to increase the scope of communication within the mainstream of social-
science research. While many of the examples are taken from "adult"
education as well as the resource specializations, other communicators
will find the approach particularly appropriate to a wide range of human
development professions.

Communications specialists will look to this approach in order to
conceive of their professional difficulties in communication terms and
realize that encounter negotiation and information surprise are the fundamental components of relevance. In general, the many exercises and
simulations are designed to be readily understood by and acceptable to
staff members, while at the same time avoiding the limitation of single
examples without a conceptual framework. The professional methods
of human communication are presented within the psychology of the behavioral cycle. Human-relations training, group dynamics, and decision
making are immersed in small-group sociology. Community psychology
and coordination support the professional methods of persuasion, mass
communication, advocacy, and community development.

PREFACE

This publication lays a foundation of communications training for resource specialists and is designed to enable them to assess the processes and behaviors inherent in a transactional environment, the consequences of these interactions with other phenomena, as well as the way they react on human behavior. Any change in the content of information stimuli and in the negotiation of message space alters individual personality, and, ultimately, the nature of human society. The methods of interface, together with their embedded techniques as developed in this publication, are designed to serve the social objectives of media, library and information science, and technology.

Throughout the country, resource specialists are disturbed and perplexed by the "bold new approach" to the evaluation of media and library and information service called for in patterns of citizen involvement and local control. The core of the problem includes these imperatives: to integrate resource-center service with the community; to focus attention upon current social needs; to make the full range of information and communicative help which the community has to offer readily to persons in need; to increase the likelihood that concerns can be identified and help provided early enough to do some good; to strengthen the service program of the community resource agency for the prevention of information dislocation.

In much agency-community relations, there is a tendency to rush into ill-conceived publicity programs rather than give the neighborhoods and their groups enough time to become aware of, and informed about, deep community concerns and to discuss their purposes and interests in relation to relevant program development. This approach to community development will help resource specialists to develop an understanding of group- and power-structure characteristics as well as of the abilities required to service people's needs and interests. It is the basis for any community development enterprise contrived for the educational and informational enterprise.

The national effort to improve the quality of life for every individual, i.e., to alleviate poverty, to improve educational opportunities, to combat lack of information access, etc., have already begun to tax the

resources of professional manpower. In spite of expanded imperatives
to understand and facilitate the process of change, from group discussion
to community action, the communication programs of media, library
and information centers face growing shortages of technically-skilled
personnel who are also expert in community development. Most critical of all is the lack of ability to relate information to the dynamics of
encounter situations.

Efforts towards the collection and organization of the nonverbal and
audiovisual message space of the people are today in many communities
under development. The numerous hot lines and various neighborhood
information centers have begun the task of organizing the informal information networks, "talking chains," of the people. These endeavors
witness the fact that much wisdom, value, and skill exist within people
and only await the organizing and indexing ability which one would expect to find among resource specialists if they would only put their efforts to work in community development.

The means are available to help resource specialists break the
confines of limited helpfulness and involve a wide range of citizens in
describing and recording the nonverbal and audiovisual message space
within which they are emersed. Oral history, local wisdom, and neighborhood "technology" could be recorded on film or videotapes and possibly written in some instances. At the least, records of where to go
for local information could be developed in order to make wider access
possible. Community resource persons who have the sanction of the
people could be indexed and their competencies related to the specialties
of others.

In general, the community is a large and amorphous entity with
which it is difficult if not impossible to work. In this volume, systematic
plans are presented for the articulation and analysis of concerns and
interests which, in turn, can be employed as guidelines for program and
message design.

Had librarians more generally risen to the opportunity offered to
them by the Library-Community Project of the American Library
Association, the sudden transition to the present decade of accountability
and lay control might have been more developmental and educational
for a wider range of citizen volunteers. Instead of being forced into
violent administrative confrontation with activists, the community-library
relations could, based upon the principles and methods presented here,
become a behavioral environment programmed for discovery learning.

Certainly the methods and program of agency-community development
when implemented by resource communicators will create the conditions
wherein all citizens can continue their own self-development and education.

The underlying causes for consumer action can be investigated by
methods more sophisticated than those which assume that consumers
understand and can identify the causes of their own actions. In any event
the principle holds: that which makes a community change are articulated
concerns and interests. This is especially to be kept in mind when making
a community study, where the temptation may be strong to get the survey done as quickly and "efficiently" as possible.

Community development as a communicative method, together with
its associated study design, is employed in order to involve volunteers
in continuing, self-educational activities. Guidelines are presented for
the professional staff who must undertake widespread and continuous recruitment and sponsor group programs of a high order of communicative
effectiveness.

The citizen activist will find much to support his conviction that
resource access should be more widely available to all people. Guidelines are presented that will help him evaluate not only the programs
of a single agency but also the effective liaison of one agency with another.
The functions of a coordinating structure provide a framework within
which to examine the communications and information-processing systems of the community. In order that this general procedure be acceptable to the people, methods are presented so that it can be worked out
based upon the identified goals of the community.

People are everywhere emersed in the wisdom, the values, and
the skills of their culture. They constantly seek access to local resources which, too frequently, are inadequately organized for use.
The concept and functions of community information centers whether
for crisis intervention, counseling, or referral can now be considered
within the framework of peoples' use patterns whether as citizens or
as resource-agency patrons.

The traditional model of service, that based upon reading as the
ideal intrapersonal communication, is still beyond the reach of many
citizens. Communication on the other hand is an interactive and transactional bargaining process carried on in order to satisfy personal
concerns and interests. This general need for a helping profession

in the community has been translated into responsive methods and motivational devices by means of which relationships can be created between
knowledge and information and the concerns and interests of people.

Resource specialists need training not only in community development but particularly in enhancing the performance of resource-center
personnel and in preparing them to cope with the real world of urban
policies and urban structure. Media and information service should be
effective enough to coordinate community information dissemination as
well as to develop services of interest and relevance to all citizens.
This is all the more urgent in an era when the problems of the urban
core demand the most effective dissemination of information and the
development of community-related services of superior performance.

The forces of professional orthodoxy and the apparent lack of public
initiative must be counteracted in order to involve all citizens, including
the poor and uneducated, in the processes of determining information
policy in the community. If the patron is poor, undereducated, and non-
vocal he is usually given brief and mechanical access to books that will
pass his time, e. g., traditional outreach programs. On the other hand
if his socioeconomic and educational position is more favorable, he is
more likely to receive long-term literature searches and subject analyses
relevant to his personal interest.

Inventiveness and research are needed, a position which this work
boldly asserts based upon the principles and significant applications to
media, library, and information science. Still other innovations, more
radical in their departures from the traditional approach, will be required
if the major institutional setting of youth and adult like, school and job,
are to be modified in ways that promote the constructive handling of life
stresses on the part of large numbers of people. Those professionals
who are responsible for in-service training will find many ideas of value
in preparing staff to serve the community as catalysts in order to promote the identification of group interests and problems, the use of ex-
hibitions and other educational strategies for citizen involvement, and
to muster liaison with a wide range of community resources as well as
to understand that funding for resource service is a commitment of the
total community.

This text will help specialists in media and library and information
science to undertake more extensive field-research programs. The advantages of on-going urban situations lie in the built-in stimuli to inquiry
and the much larger repertoire of types of studies which become possible.

Conceptualized as a communication and learning environment, research
in dynamic situations can involve long-range experimentation in the development of evaluative and measurement devices whose results are
more accurately predictive. Among the other advantages of field research which this publication supports, the following may serve as examples:

A new impetus in giving communication services explicit form
as a major professional area based upon concepts and ideas,
i.e., models, based on the findings of social-science research.

A central thrust to the development and evaluation of new program ideas and new methods of motivating participation and
learning. Problems in community development, while not
absent from rural settings, are most crucial today in the urban community.

A focus of attention on the need for a long range systematic
research program using new methods and techniques of research as a basis for effective planning in communication
services.

Development and validation of investigation techniques which
minimize error and maximize yield of information for both
research in the laboratory and evaluation of dynamic communications situations.

A raised communicative potential of the individual citizen by
means of increased professional competence in dyad, group
and community contexts.

Address the issues of intercultural diversity and analyze
the problems of crosscultural communication.

Support for important policy decisions confronting community
leaders regarding totally mediated environments under both
computer and upchannel audio-video control.

In understanding community psychology and coordination the resource specialist and other related professionals can support the continuing learning projects of a wide range of citizen interests and levels
of entry. With this approach, the communicator can create the conditions
for a "life curriculum" by means of which the citizen can process in-

formation relevant to the transactional nature of his environment. A citizen involved with real-life negotiations considers knowledge more from its transactional value than in terms of the subject orientation so typical of organized materials collections.

CONTENTS

COMMUNITY
PSYCHOLOGY AND
COORDINATION

ONE

INTRODUCTION

Communication is a process of change for both sender and receiver. Everyone who communicates does so because he wants to affect human behavior for the better and grow and develop as a person himself in the process.

When a communicator goes into service in a particular community, his success depends to a great extent upon how well he can initially analyze and interpret three major factors: the situation in relation to his specialty; the people involved in the situation; and himself with respect to the situation and the people involved.

No matter how familiar the communicator may be with media, library and information agencies and their services, he will find it profitable to examine the total environment within which his agency operates. New experiences and knowledge will suggest new things to look for, and as a result he will be able to inquire, interpret or explain events in new ways. In other words he will more easily articulate the unspoken concerns and interests of the citizens.

It is important to try to determine why conditions are as they are before attempting to initiate any changes. Surface explanations or excuses for the status quo may be interesting but they seldom represent probes into basic problems. People usually need help in articulating explanations which lie below the surface of banal criticism and rationalization. Criticism is the first articulation in the process of being able to identify that a problem exists and is usually based on feelings and intuition. Frequently, criticism does not represent the "real" problem but simply may be taken as evidence that a real problem may exist.

It is easy for example in agency-community relations to listen to and accept such explanations as "insufficient funds," or "lack of trained personnel." It is more difficult, but surely more rewarding, to analyze the current utilization of resources and determine whether other courses of action are available. Such a course of action will require considerable analysis of community reports and much thinking and discussion. But

this is the role of a communicator working to articulate the unspoken
concerns and interests of citizens.

The nature, direction and extent of change that may be taking place
in the community can be observed, discussed, and articulated. Any
change is initiated by certain groups of people in an attempt to offset
particular problems. Perhaps the most obvious indication of such
developments may be changes in agency and organizational personnel as
well as new roles in the community in which public figures and emerging
leaders are involved. Social, political, or technological changes may
have increased or decreased the importance of some agency or specific
parts of it. In the presence of this change, what problems and opportunities have arisen which may need to be taken into account in adjusting
the expectations which any communicator may have?

The formal structure of agency community relations should be
studied and analyzed. How are decisions made? Who makes them?
What are the guidelines used in decision making? There may be a fixed
and inflexible pattern for deploying materials and personnel which stems
from a power center above each agency. Or it may be that the citizen
board members of the communicator's agency have enough stature and
power to permit the development of a coordinating community structure
which could serve the concerns of a wide range of citizen interests.

Within the system in which a communicator operates, there are
specific groups of people with whom the communicator must work if his
ideas are to be successfully received. These "audiences" will probably
be relatively small face-to-face groups of individuals with varying degrees of influence over other citizens. It is necessary to proceed
slowly and observe carefully the effects of the ideas which the communicator has articulated.

Whatever the plan, it involves new ways of behaving for the citizens
involved. People tend to place high value on the knowledge, skills, and
beliefs which they have acquired. The ideas proposed may seem to
attack these values, either by implication or directly. Colleagues and
citizens will be willing to accept new ideas only if presented in ways consistent with their values, or if they can substitute new values of a higher
order to themselves, to the agency or to the community.

Any audience considering newly articulated proposals will make
such changes only to the extent that they are ready and able to make
them. They need to be made thoroughly aware of present unsatisfactory

conditions and to become familiar with desirable alternatives. The communicator must carefully observe their readiness to change as well as their acceptance of what has already been accomplished. It may be necessary to break up new ideas into many small ideas and to observe carefully what happens before, during, and after each one in order to determine how to proceed. Plans and goals may need to be modified many times as the result of continuous observation.

No inventory of factors of success is complete without an attempt by the agent of change to describe himself and his role in the community. Has he acquired the knowledge and ability to accomplish what is desirable, or is a lack of technique likely to betray him once the program is undertaken? Can he place himself in the role of listener and observer? Does he feel obliged to criticize those who disagree with him rather than to understand their view and reconcile it with his own? Does he have an honest picture of how to get along with his associates? Can he remedy those personal factors which seem to interfere with good relationships between himself and those around him? Does he have a deep commitment to those goals and programs in which he is involved? Can he formulate strategies to utilize communication channels and data to meet the goals and objectives set forth?

*   *   *

The community may at first appear to be an extremely frustrating context within which to take action. But the communicator in media, library and information science has a systematic and operational approach to community development. There are in general three major and interdependent roles which a communicator can play in the community enterprise:

Articulation of the concerns and interests of citizens which remain on an informal level of awareness.

Program development in areas of concern and interest in order to bring them into formal awareness of citizens and involve them in exploratory and solution experience.

Resource coordination so that materials, facilities, and technologies can be effectively deployed by a wide range of professional personnel.

ARTICULATION OF CONCERNS AND INTERESTS

The concerns and interests of people may be stimulated by any sector of community life. But while environmental conditions may constitute the precipitating causes of many needs, the real concern or interest arises in the minds of people. At first, the concern may be only an inchoate feeling of uneasiness buried under attitudes and predispositions which has to be nurtured into cognitive awareness by the communicator. The communicator must himself be aware of the people in order to phrase their concerns and interests in concepts and terminology which can be readily understood.

Population data helps to predict future trends. When a much larger number of males or females exist in a population grouping, the sex mores and behavior will probably differ from those where the ratio is more evenly balanced. The adjustment of a community to such imbalance may influence to a considerable degree the content of programs or even the time of day at which such activities might be offered.

The number and kind of people in a community influence social living. In general the degree of concentration of people in a given area, the greater the degree of specialization. High population density indicates a greater degree of specialization, and means that people will be less well acquainted with others in their immediate vicinity. A prevailing high degree of specialization will influence program design, while comparative isolation makes participation and involvement in the program more difficult to achieve.

Where the community is homogeneous, e.g., white, native born and long-time residents, program planning and communication are comparatively simple. But where concentrations or "colonies" of race and nationality groups establish themselves at various points, the job of building a "community" program becomes more difficult. The agency educator must know the proportion of each segment and the areas of concentration. Distinctive mores, customs, and living conditions must be determined in order to discern ways and means in which the program may serve these groups.

Programs of various social agencies in the community are affected by changes in population, size, and characteristics. The age and sex of the population may greatly affect the community's organized life. For instance, many rural communities have a comparatively high proportion of very young and very old people. This places a heavy economic burden upon the community. Such a population structure materially limits the communications and educational programs to those activities which meet the needs and interests of older people.

The present life of any community can be understood better when viewed against its historical perspective. Historical facts can become the motivating force for community improvement programs. On the other hand, the strength of traditions and cleavages in the past sometimes prevent efficient and necessary solutions. The communicator must distinguish between those that have grown out of past history, and those that have been acquired in more recent times.

In some instances, however, a community may have too little sense of continuity with the past. Consequently it lacks any motivating force to build stability and morale essential to mutual activity. Geographic factors are easy to overlook in the development of community life. A particular type of soil, certain minerals in the earth, the junction of rivers, natural harbors, or special scenic attractions may have crucial significance in forming the community. Such factors can influence the size and character of the population and determine its industries.

Communities are characterized by things in which people are interested: the situations, qualities, or conditions they value. Such community values are hard to identify. But they are important to anyone who is trying to work professionally with the community in any type of informational, educational, or action program. Communications and programs are doomed when they simply do not fit into dominant value patterns in the community. The communicator must identify basic values and build his program in terms of them.

PROGRAM DEVELOPMENT

The development of relevant communication programs is based in the surprise value of the information presented. In order to facilitate access to information, it is important to understand the underlying information structure of the community. In most societal contexts, from the primitive to the highly complex modern civilizations, it can be hypothesized that four social methods of communication exist. Scholarship or knowledge is communicated through these general social methods. This is of course not meant to imply that knowledge is necessarily made kinetic or active by any one or all of these methods. Information surprises may occur, but to plan for their occurrence is the function of a situations-producing theory of communication.

Mass media provide a rain of data which arouse interests and problems in the minds of people and help them to articulate the concerns which exist nowhere except in their own minds. Mass communication

makes it possible for every citizen to be continuously exposed to a rain
of information concerning current happenings and to a hail of arguments
or suggestions intended to confirm or alter convictions. Orchestration
of media around significant concerns and interests makes it difficult for
citizens to avoid thinking about important community issues. It should
be kept in mind that each individual places highest values on those issues which he sees as directly affecting himself. Unless the issues are
presented in such a context, they will not seem relevant to him.

Mass media contribute to and communicate the knowledge of the
present moment, the near past, and the impending future. The emerging
needs of the people help to shape the sources of information readily
available even though there are but few citizens in the area who are especially motivated to seek them out. The general public is largely satisfied with the program content of the mass media. However, specialists need information in order to anticipate media programming several
weeks or possibly months ahead and to assemble resources that will
extend and deepen media impact when it occurs.

Educational experiences are provided in a variety of traditional
ways such as the school, the resource, and continuing educational
agencies. More recently however, there is a considerable groundswell
of interest in having the total community programmed for continuous
learning through involvement. The general method is known as the community development enterprise. Education is, of course, used in its
broadest sense, including adult education, as a method whereby the common scholarship required by every citizen and especially those in
specialized vocations are explicitly educated. Counseling is used frequently in the endeavor for cognitive development and cognitive flexibility.

A good amount of knowledge, particularly that related to the educational and work-a-day life of people, exists in records and sources
that are ephemeral and not highly organized, or perhaps remain unorganized. This type of knowledge is often mission-oriented, as for
example, a lettuce or grape growers boycott information center. Information is retrieved from such sources only so long as there is an
obvious and continuing need and often for a limited clientele. So far,
resource agencies such as media, library, and information centers
with limited support have been able to acquire and store only the more
structured resources and materials which have a greater probable
potentiality for continuing information retrieval and which are oriented
to the past as opposed to the present or future.

Consultation is the general method whereby knowledge is made kinetic in the lives of people who are motivated to seek out a member of a helping profession. Consultation processes are used by such learned professions as medicine, law, and engineering. A sick person or one involved in a lawsuit, does not read a medical or legal treatise. Instead he consults a physician or lawyer to obtain the particular bits of professional scholarship applicable to his case. Community referral is an area of concern to librarians serving in community coordinating structures or libraries as a method for making knowledge kinetic in the lives of people.

This extensive category of knowledge does not exist in records at all, but is stored largely in the minds of specialists and professional experts. This type of knowledge becomes available only upon consultation. The information is rendered kinetic, for example, when the individual interfaces with a consulting expert over an immediate problem or specific interest. Resource control in such instances constitutes an identification of consultants and an awareness of the scope and availability of their expertise. The number of community referral agencies is increasing as, for example, the information "hotlines" and information bureaus.

Retrieval access is the method whereby the individual extracts the exact piece of scholarship needed at any moment from a group of documents or related materials although the exact knowledge is explicitly contained in no one of them. Finding and reading a single volume on a desired topic is but a truncated form of the complete reference process.

Characteristic of most metropolitan areas, the urban community is rich in information resources, both general and specialized. The major resource centers such as media, library, and information agencies have sometimes begun to work together in something resembling a regional information center in order to avoid unnecessary duplication of resource collections and to facilitate access both to their own resources and to other agencies in the national network.

There are many resource agencies in the metropolitan area which have not undertaken formal membership in the regional center. Numerous other information centers exist which function as significant services to specialized interests. All of these benefit in varying degrees from the information transfer (bibliographic) network. Many of these agencies service a common set of community needs for information, while others service concerns and interests which cannot be met from documents that stem from the usual publishing and distribution channels.

There are many unmet needs for information which exist in metropolitan areas. A few directories are available; some are more structured than others as is the case with library catalogs of holdings. The
coordination of complete bibliographic access is an extensive and expensive process, and in many instances may provide a range of detail
that is beyond the information space being negotiated for a request.
Perhaps only the very specialized request requires the exhaustive
treatment which complete bibliographic access is designed to meet.

However, this type of request, while the major preoccupation of
present day library service, represents but a fraction of the total information needs of the people in a community. Their requirements
are conditioned partially by the media and partially by their daily occupations. Consequently, the information spaces sought range widely
over ephemeral and mission oriented sources of knowledge. Only a
small percentage of the information required every day is sought in
the depth which the bibliographic record and the indexed knowledge
store are designed to serve. Of course without such inquiry from the
record, civilization would flounder for lack of perspective. In the
long run, libraries of the record are an integral element of modern
vigorous civilizations, but in the day to day preoccupations of people
they often seem irrelevant.

RESOURCE COORDINATION

The coordination of resources and the deployment of technology
are large and pervasive factors in any community enterprise. Although much of the endeavor is borne by private enterprise, it is the
values and concerns of the citizenry which establish the broad guidelines within which technology and resources are deployed. Government
is the basic vehicle through which the will of the people is made manifest.

The communicator will not have much influence and his programs
will not be implemented unless they appear to be compatible with prevailing economic and governmental endeavors. Indeed, government
cannot tolerate any coalition stronger than itself and as a result has
final jurisdiction over legislation and public funding. This is an important consideration at a time in most communities when private and
philanthropic funding is extremely limited. On the other hand, public
funding is also curtailed and can only be expanded to the extent that

citizens are willing to pay for increased communication and information programs.

Local government is of interest to everyone. It speaks for and affects the entire community. It relates to the health, education, and welfare of all citizens. During recent years its activities in these areas have markedly increased. The agency educator should continuously study local government in order that his communication and program may deal with timely activities. This will bring increased knowledge of government to the people, and prepare them to participate more fully in the solution of current social problems.

An interest in government is usually not lacking among the people of a community. What is lacking all too often is the knowledge of just how individuals can make their thinking known about governmental affairs and contribute to the shaping of community policy. Here is where agency communication and education can make a valuable contribution. Timely communications and programs may bring individuals together for discussion sessions with government officials and leaders in the community. Communications and educational programs can then function for the improvement of the democratic process. Better understanding can be gained of the many processes for democratic government. More participation, and more enlightened participation will result.

The economic structure determines the level of community living, the breadth and depth of community activities. It provides the means by which people meet their basic needs for food, clothing, and shelter. It determines the extent to which they can go beyond that point and ultimately carry heavier tax burdens. Large scale production, new materials, the increase of capital, development of completely new industries, the shifting of labor forces, new patterns of employer- employee relationships, changes in markets and legislative controls, and transportation are some of the problems associated with the many-sided business of making a living.

As the population increases, greater varieties and amounts of goods are needed and more services of various kinds are required. Relationships of individuals even within a single occupation tend to become indirect. It becomes increasingly difficult to evaluate the activity of one population segment in comparison with others. Such a condition favors the development of special interest segments out of which organizations are formed to promote such special interests. The adult educator must design his program to serve the needs of these specialized groups.

The educational level of the population influences community welfare, particularly its civic, social, and vocational aspects. Participation in community affairs is highly correlated with level of formal education. The higher the level of education, the greater the extent of participation. The nature and structure of community organizations, and patterns of affiliation, are strongly influenced by levels of education. Uneducated, unskilled persons live differently (in many respects) from more highly educated industrial technicians and professional persons. The adult education program will necessarily vary accordingly.

The economic structure of a community often produces more problems than any other segment of community life. The agency educator's job is to identify and understand the problems that exist within the economic structure of his community, and to deal with these problems through the machinery of communication and education. Unemployment, poverty, insecurity, exploitation of labor, waste of natural resources, labor-management conflicts, and the inadequate production to meet community needs are some of the problems which can be reduced or kept to a minimum only through continuing study and cooperative action on the part of individuals and group.

An atmosphere should be created in which such problems can be faced realistically and worked out democratically by community groups. Continuing liaison, cooperative study, and discussion helps the agency educator learn of industry's personnel needs, training, and retraining requirements, and plans for expansion of plants. Industry learns how communication and education may serve these needs. The education of adults and the improvement of community living is a cooperative social process. Nowhere is cooperative action more important than in the training of people for business and industry through continuing education.

It is hypothesized that as communication and information facilities become more evenly distributed to various classes of people, the educational process will change from its present content orientation to a process orientation. In such a mode, people can learn how to process information via various communication channels and with a variety of techniques rather than continue to memorize facts.

QUESTION ANALYSIS AND DISCUSSION

The questions which appear below are designed for analysis and discussion. The questions have been validated in the theories and systems principles, which support media, library and information science (101). They have been phrased in a way, hopefully, which can lead to verification within the service enterprise of the communicator.

These guide questions may be kept in mind while reading the text, or considered as points for reflection after an initial reading. No question is keyed to any single chapter or particular section of it. In general, the questions can only be answered to the reader's satisfaction after reading, reflection, and analysis of the entire work:

How well are specialists in media, library, and information science using the models of community development and mass communication in order to promote community service? What is the relationship of community activity to group and individual activity? How is interpersonal transition effected? For what reasons and how are individuals and groups counseled to participate in community activity?

What is the communicator's orientation to the community? Are the needs and values, for which information is sought, determined by the community and dependent upon its initiative? If so, is the communicator but a "bookstore" manager to the community?

What is the relationship of the social myths (edenic and utopian) to the community objectives not being met? How does the communicator exploit the social myths for community betterment through effective service?

How does the communicator involve the people in consensus-making and anticipate their decisions while making certain that citizens feel themselves to be in the "drivers seat" of community affairs?

How are the elements of a situation-producing theory of communication (agent, patron, situation, goal, policy, motivation) institutionalized and implemented by the communicator in the community?

Compare and contrast the development of public relations
with the communicative role of the media center in the
community. How are the mass media employed in each
instance?

How are sociodrama (games, demonstrations, spectacles),
knowledge generation (are disciplines led by profession?)
and community development (community study) used as alternative methods (or in combinations) for the community
to consider, and why?

How are communities exposed to information so that communication may occur? Specifically, how is information
retrieval done for the community?

Compare and contrast the roles of "objectivity" versus
"advocacy" in developing community based media services.
What are their historical antecedents of the profession,
and specifically of the center's role as a coordinating
structure in the community?

TWO

COMMUNITY IMPERATIVES

Large scale economic and social organization, the extension of
state control, and the centralization of technology have made it almost
impossible for any single individual to control these movements by himself alone and exploit them for his own purposes. Even the regional
folk cultures have been orchestrated into a mass society where the
media of communication articulate the concerns and interests of all the
people, move them towards a formal awareness of social problems and
motivate the scientific community to create a technology that will provide a sheltered environment for all citizens. Of course as always,
there are many prophets of doom who can see nothing in these sweeping
social transformations but the development of human beehives.

Despite gloomy observations and obvious present conditions it may
not be beyond the bounds of possibility to build a cultural tradition that
has integrity and authority for the general public, especially if social
agencies like the centers of media, library, and information resources
will work to establish an interface with the community whereby individual citizens can participate more effectively in policy decisions which
affect the entire community. Voluntary initiative can be encouraged
alongside and within the public administration of various agencies.
The professional staff of resource centers can encourage neighborhood
activities of all kinds and thus create opportunities for responsible and
voluntary initiative. Such activities could include formal and informal
continuing education on a sufficiently intimate scale for personal relations to count. From such voluntary groups, as basic units of democracy, the individual can then graduate to larger responsibility in the
communicative enterprise of society.

From the viewpoint of cybernetics, any large scale formal social
organization is a communication network. Local areas can be considered structurally as subsystems in a communications net. Many
channels operate in the system and thereby act as links through which
information flows into the local area from the outside world and thereby offsets its physical boundaries. This flow of information effects
the inhabitants behavior and reactions. If there are few inputs from

the outside world, the people in the subsystems will have few ideas
other than those with which they grew up. Information is, of course,
only that which is added to prior knowledge. If people have very little
prior knowledge about the world beyond their boundaries, it can be assumed that when these people have access to communication channels,
they will obtain a great amount of information and be surprised for extended periods of time.

The rate of change in the system will increase with the role of new
input information into the environment. A runaway condition can develop
in the system. The danger of it developing is always greatest and the
intensity of its occurrence varies directly with the amount of information
received. But as the educational level of the people increases through
formal and continuing education, the amount of information (new knowledge) received tends to level off with the subsequent decrease in the
danger of a runaway system developing. Consequently, the revolutionary transformations of the past century can in part be considered as an
index of successful introduction and operation of widespread communications technology.

The focal point of most citizens' awareness today is not some communal area such as the market place or a building for religious worship
as it used to be in the past, but the media of communication with which
he can interface at any point and be perfectly at home. The citizen no
longer needs to travel to a gathering place to meet and talk; he can do
so at any point in the communication system. As a result, except for
the transporting of artifacts, food and wastes, national and international
transportation systems will have to be replanned and redeveloped (50).
This is evident today with an energy crisis and the maze of transportation
related problems facing the United States. The movement from physical
to mediated contact among people is as real as and possibly more revolutionary than the rural-urban changes of the past half century.

In any event, the mediated community is rapidly replacing the urban or suburban community and has already begun to provide many opportunities and expectations for human interrelationship. Larger projects and increased social power bring together an increasing number
of human beings, all of whom are planners, sources, and users of information and energy. The trend towards interdependency which is
rapidly increasing has already tied together greater numbers of people
in more intimate ways than in previous social periods. In a democratic
society, power becomes a shared control: shared purposes, rights,
and responsibilities. The intimacy of interpersonal relationships will

deepen and widen and communications will play an increasingly decisive role.

COMMUNITY ORGANIZATION

Community organization is a network of relationships which exist in any social structure. No person or agency lives for itself alone but always as a member of a group and a community. Community organization is a process through which human relationships are initiated, altered, or terminated to meet changing conditions. Cooperative effort is a significant process by means of which people grow in insight and ability. The local community and now in particular the mediated community is a laboratory where citizens can learn the reserve, good will, and scientific attitude needed to resolve personal and group differences.

Mediated communities provide opportunities for promoting democratic methods as well as situations where people can learn to resolve differences. In working together, citizens not only build things but also people and their characters. Since public opinion is formed in interpersonal interaction, citizens cannot afford to become complacent about values in community life. Self reliance is fostered by success. Some things can be done best by the federal government, others by state government, and still many others through local initiative. Citizens learn to use resources from outside instead of passively submitting to them.

At first, whenever cooperative effort is required, people tend to react according to special interest. Since vested interest groups are the common denominator of community life, broad communicative efforts are needed to reconcile divergent viewpoints. Diversity of economic interests, and of cultural and religious groups is a reflection of similar diversity on the national and international levels. The mediated community is an ideal assemblage in which to come to grips with the crucial problems of local, national and international communities. National and world problems can be seen to better advantage and be dealt with more realistically.

For some, however, the mediated community is the beginning of the end for the individual person. They see only that there is a rapidly increasing number of human beings who can interfere with them or who may be needed in the negotiation of any one individual's plans. Many people impinge upon the individual and seek help from him in the execution

of their plans. For any individual human being there is wider opportunity for control and for being controlled because power in the affairs of
men is supposed to accrue to those who can supply the wants of others.
But as the function of communication continues to expand, the number
of opportunities for the individual as an institution increase. The individual has not been passed over by the huge corporations of the postindus-
trial state. In reality, "it is he who has passed over the institutions of
corporation, university, novel and play to become an institution in himself (137)."

Such a concept as the institutionalization of the individual is not
new. Katz (68) called the phenomenon personal influence in attempting
to establish the relationship between the media of communication and
public opinion. On the other hand, Hall (54) has described it as the process of social perception in which the communications leaders move
society from informal through formal and into technological awareness.
The media not only survey the environment but also and probably of more
significance they articulate the concerns and interests of the citizens.
A quarter of a century ago, these functions were identified by the Commission on Freedom of the Press (27):

Provide full access to the day's intelligence.

Present a comprehensive account of the day's
events in a context which gives them meaning.

Serve as a forum for the exchange of comment
and criticism.

Represent the constituent groups in society.

Clarify the goals and values of society.

The media of communication are increasingly being orchestrated
around social issues in order to serve the functions of society. The
content of messages through the communications media is closely related to individuals, situations, and the group environment. Of course
the individual will have to share control over the messages, the situations, and the group environment or else he will be submerged in and
at the mercy of centralized control. The individual must preserve his
freedom and help others control themselves through community enterprise, institutions, and agencies, as well as the many voluntary organizations. Although they have significant differences because of special-

ized roles, the people in a community have enough in common to work together. In fact there must be considerable appreciation of a commonness of kind in order that a maximum number of individuals can realize themselves in society. A communications network must be available for the greatest number of individuals to participate for their own advantage.

In addition to the rapidly increasing complexity in the intersections of human behavior, there is a growing complexity of message space. So rapid has the increased complexity become that many have labelled the exponential rise as an "information explosion." Indeed contemporary man, at least in the western democracies, is almost saturated in his message space particularly with messages of the present moment. In the past, human satisfaction and individual development were largely facilitated in voluntary groups and activities concentrated in one location. Notices were sent out through the newspaper for time and place of assembly. Today with the channel capacity of the videophone and cablevision it is possible to assemble a group upon a moment's notice wherever the individuals happen to be. Nor does the wired group have to suspend deliberations and reassemble for decision making. Computer assisted delphi techniques can facilitate the decision making process via the same display console.

The totality of the interrelationships in the message space have become exceedingly complex. No one individual or even a group of individuals can keep all of message space under surveillance. Some system of interlocking subsystems is required which will be responsive to the citizen's concerns and interests on a dynamic and interactive basis. In response to this social imperative, Lacy (72) has identified the general functions of an interlocking communications lattice:

> Record and organize for recall the increasing
> number of elements in knowledge which must be
> handled individually and in relation to all other
> elements.

> Convey to a mass audience information of such
> complexity as has previously only been received
> by a small, elite group.

> Promote the continuing development and the
> reeducation of all citizens.

Provide news coverage in greater depth and
complexity for the numbers of people to be
kept informed.

Increase the opportunity for minority, divergent,
and critical comment.

Promote experimental approaches to problem
solving in order to close the gap between
scientific and technological developments, and
governmental and institutional change.

SYSTEMS TECHNOLOGY

The requirements of Lacy's system can only be met by the com-
plexities of an advanced communications technology. But the demands
of such a system are probably no more difficult than the effort required
to place man on the moon. The space program was a social demonstration
of the feasibility of bringing together segments of the intellectual, industrial, and technological communities needed to fulfill goals in a timely
fashion. The formula that worked for NASA is clear and straightforward
(50):

Identify clearcut goals.

Institutionalize the mechanisms for achieving
these goals.

Engage all segments of society whose talents
and resources are needed to fulfill these goals.

Create a market to receive the new output and
new technology.

The formula, if it can be called such, is really systems analysis
and design which is already being employed in various kinds of ways.
People are becoming familiar with projections about the impact of processes such as cybernation or the combination of computer and automa-
tion technology. The point has already been reached where the actual
manufacture or creation of economic goods is no longer a very significant problem in society. Goods can be produced so rapidly that the problems of creating human needs to use these materials is becoming more
significant than the problem of creating the goods themselves. Develop-

ments such as these and others are rapidly changing previously held concepts of the physical community and community services.

Systems analysis and design technology gives promise of accomplishing things which a very short time ago would have been viewed as completely impossible. With the application of systems analysis techniques to community affairs, the level of expectation has risen and the range of what man can conceive as within the range of possibility has widened considerably. Mankind is moving out of the old horizons of human possibilities in fantastic and even frightening ways by combining the highly sophisticated systems analysis and design approaches to the managing, planning, and utilization of human resources. Many of these approaches will be used in solving some of the kinds of social and human problems that confront society.

Social engineering or environmental design has also had an impact on the community. A sophisticated technology is becoming available in order to design total human environments in ways that will have a profound impact on the behavior of people living in those environments. One of the things which has come to be understood about human behavior in the past few years is the fact that a great deal of human behavior is the product of immediate environmental forces operating in the perceptual field or stimulus situation of an individual. Society is beginning to learn how to design and program these environments in order to produce predictable kinds of behavior in people. The ability to make tremendous multimedia inputs into the human being in a controlled environment will be expanded more than is presently realized.

The ability has been developed to engineer human beings biologically in ways not dreamed about before. Biological engineering has already created tremendous possibilities and many problems. The field of organ transplants, for example, has shown some of the horizons that lie before mankind. It is possible to create spare parts for human beings. To use these with any degree of control is a problem that society has not yet come close to solving. The kinds of responsibilities that go along with these possibilities may be frightening to some. One example of this responsibility lies in the area of using transplanted organs from a human donor. The question concerning when the donor is legally dead has caused serious problems of control. Although the human genetic structure which was sabotaged with radioactivity in the last few years has been to an extent controlled, society continues to permit chemical pollution. This occurs because society has not accepted responsibility for social control.

The effects of the cybernetic revolution have not been adequately
assessed. Society is limited not so much by a lack of potential talent
as by the ability to envision the kind of environments which can be
developed and then make an effort to muster the technology. The resource professions of media, library, and information science have a
considerable responsibility to articulate this concern unless they de-
cide to abdicate their role in the communications enterprise. Leaders
in these professions will tend to work longer hours and have their life
styles involved more directly in professional roles. This type of individual and his wife will be centrally involved in a process where work,
continuing education, and leisure become inseperable. The demands
for such resource persons will be almost insatiable in the future communications systems.

On the other hand, society will soon have some unknown but large
percentage of the population who will increasingly find that their life
styles and ways of organizing their lives are related only in very tenuous ways to the work life. Work will not be a very central part of
one's life style. The amount of work in society that is meaningful, or
rewarding in some psychological sense in itself has been shrinking for
many years. Many people will simply have to find other ways to develop
an identity and a satisfying total life style than through work.

Very often people who by virtue of their background are least able
to handle large amounts of leisure time, have the most time available
to them. Many of these people have had to find alternative ways to establish feelings of self worth and personal identity as their career
styles diminish in importance. One of the things that may happen is
that serial careers will become the norm. People will have several
different careers at different stages in their lives. Rather than
having a simple straight line career pattern, people will change dras-
tically the kind of work they do in a lifetime at least two or three times.

STIMULUS HUNGER

Another part of this process is the rising tide of expectations that
people have in society. Society is demanding a life style that is psychologically rich and meaningful, as well as materially rich. Economic
expectations are obviously on the rise. It seems that the capacity is
available, if not the wisdom, to meet those expectations. The average
real wage, in spite of creeping inflation, may almost double during the
next decade, that is the purchasing power of people may virtually
double. The technological capacity to eliminate poverty is available,

whether or not the social engineering capacity to do so can be mustered.

A generation has been created that is hungry for meaningful kinds of psychological experiences. Much of the dropout phenomenon among college students and the young generally may be a reaction that is really based on an increasing level of expectations about what life should bring. Society is going to have to reorganize resources to provide richer kinds of experiences. This can be seen in a variety of forms, including the phenomenon which is known as group dynamics. The sensitivity training and intimacy kinds of experiences that seem to be tremendously popular now are examples of this striving to find meaningful relationships with people that are not available in the normal environment.

Related to this is a revision in the whole concept of what human motivation is like. Society is going to have to restructure the way people think about human motivation to understand the needs that are now being voiced in society. Concepts of human motivation in the past have been based on the psychology of scarcity with which man has lived since the beginning of recorded history. The common model of human motivation involves tension and need reduction. Motivated human activity has largely been based on the desire to reduce tension or reduce basic physiological kinds of needs. Acquiring food, shelter, and clothing have activated most of the human race for as long as evidence is available about what life has been like and still concern a considerable part of the world's population.

In an affluent society, however, the models of need reduction or tension reduction do not seem to be adequate in order to understand current human motivation. Today people have stimulus hunger and the level of stimulation that exists in an environment is an important determinate of behavior. The need to increase levels of stimulation in the environment is just as real as is the need to get food or to reduce the older kind of drives that have been known. This kind of stimulus hunger must be satisfied in the developmental history of an organism or it does not continue normal development.

A generation of people is emerging who have a higher level of stimulus hunger than most people have ever had. Part of the inability to understand social motivation stems from this phenomenon. The generation gap, for example, may be simply a difference in the level of match needed to maintain the young organism versus the old one. This mismatch is more noticeable today because of an age shift in population

in which a large percentage of people are in the 18-35 age bracket. In
past decades the majority of the population was in the over-35 age category. This delay in matching the required stimulus levels is part of
our cultural lag.

In terms of communication, this means that environments must be
designed which are richer psychologically for people. Meaningful
kinds of experiences will have to be provided for large numbers of
people at varying levels of sophistication and education. Since communities are growing more complex, professionals will increasingly
encounter people who ask to be "turned on" in some meaningful way.
Professionals will have to be the linkage between those services which
society has to offer and people who are suffering from what may be
called stimulus malnutrition, a condition which can be just as real as
many kinds of physical malnutrition. If this is not done, they are going
to build their own kinds of experiences, many of which may be potentially selfdestructive or destructive for society.

RESOURCE COORDINATION

Problems exist nowhere as much as they do in the minds of people.
The ways in which people look at and develop a solution to their problems
follow no particular patterns. There is nothing logical about problems
people have nor is there any one way in which all people solve their
problems. Although agencies exist to deal with the problems of people,
people do not always express their problems in such a way nor have the
kinds of problems for which agencies are equipped to deal. Nor for
that matter are agencies ready enough to assist people with the kinds
of problems they develop.

People with personal problems usually are not familiar with organized resources and turn to the nonverbal and audiovisual space in
which they are emersed. They take problems to friends, beauticians,
and bartenders, or else they keep them to themselves. In any event,
they get sympathy and some understanding but not very much help. If
they do go to an agency and select the wrong one for the solution of their
problem, they become frustrated and disappointed. More often than not
they get on the merry-go-round of running from agency to agency. To
be effective, a communication center must have: knowledge of resources; ability to communicate with the patron; and the ability to assist the person needing help to reach that help. The center also can
link those wishing to help others with other agencies that could use
their services and material items. As a coordinating structure, the

center also attempts to bring agencies together for an exchange of information that might result in better services to their patrons.

In any large metropolitan area there are hundreds of agencies, each with a special function. Despite the lack of coordination, most metropolitan areas are rich in information resources both general and specialized. However, persons most in need of service may not know how to find them. One central clearinghouse with widely publicized access is essential. It may make suggestions which the client can follow or make direct referrals to agencies, tax-supported or private, large or small—with suitability for helping the major criterion. Resource specialists must collect and organize information and consult with others concerned about information as well as determine the most feasible way of disseminating information. The professional communicator has to personalize the communicative situation and recognize that people do not always seek the help they need but ask about things they know.

If demand exceeds supply, resource professionals may need to motivate experts to place their knowledge in the public domain where it can be indexed for ease of access. Knowledge of the present moment, the near past and the impending future constitute an articulation of the emerging needs of the people and help to shape the information sources of the present moment. There are several media of communication in metropolis whose knowledge of the present, the near past, and the immediate future is a constant and continuous source of information which few citizens in the area could avoid even if they wanted to do so. The general public are largely satisfied with program content in the mass media and need to be motivated to think deeper about the many stimuli presented.

Consequently, there is a need in most communities for indexes and especially clearinghouses for information space that exists in ephemeral and mission-oriented sources including special libraries, information and media centers, data banks, and community resource files. The discrepancy which exists between the need for information and the efficacy with which the resource specializations make it kinetic in the affairs of citizens is approaching a crisis. If left unattended, it will be interesting to speculate on the contributory effect of a lack of available information upon the urban disorder of our time.

INVOLVEMENT AND PARTICIPATION

A democratic society depends for its existence upon citizen participation. No better way has been found to achieve widespread and enlightened citizen participation than through involvement in studying community problems and resources. It is here that communications programming comes alive, takes on real meaning and purpose for the individual,
and has considerable value for human development. Great social problems of our time are reflected in and illustrated by the context of community life. At this level, social problems can best be understood and
dealt with by the ordinary individual. Properly planned communications
and educational programs can provide the opportunity for studying these
problems and for achieving a more satisfactory understanding of them.

The community exerts a considerable influence on the development
of human personality. Together with the family, it exerts a dominant
influence on the development of attitudes, speech patterns, prejudices,
and points of view. The individual is essentially a product of the community. The communicator's chances of becoming a leader and a
guide for community development depend upon his continuous intellectual
growth and participation with others in organized community life. Communications and educational programs should become the principal medium through which this growth and development take place — an instru-
mentality for bringing about improved living in many ways.

Community development communication is a broad social endeavor
of considerable interest to institutions, agencies, and organizations.
Supported by the concept of the function of a coordinating structure, the
community enterprise achieves such order as is necessary to make it
possible for the individual citizen to enter and participate at any point
which is comfortable for him. Once involved, the individual can move
to any other point or concern of interest to him in organized message
space. The generic library composed of an information, library, and
media center is of course one of the media of communication. Unfortunately, other than in service to the individual, the library has, in the
past, been the one agency least responsive to social concerns and interests. However, the picture is gradually changing because of a recent emphasis upon community development in the profession of information, library, and media science.

Community organization is the matrix for developing purpose and
method by the resource agency, whether at the local, state or national
level. Community organization is a vertical liaison between a local

agency and its state and national affiliates as well as being a horizontal
liaison network in the local community. Community organization is a
process widely used in the network of relationships that exist in any
social structure and especially the community. No person or agency
lives for itself alone but always as a member of a group and a community. Community organization is a major method by means of which the
resource center can relate to the world around it and keep its services
geared to community needs (115):

> Our libraries are bulging with recorded knowledge,
> and we have had to invent the microfilm because we
> no longer have even space enough to store our records
> of research. Yet with all our accumulated intelli-
> gence and specialized knowledge, human beings grow
> more frustrated, problems of society multiply, and
> the mess in the world grows worse.

All resource specialists, regardless of administrative affiliation,
are required to accept the objective reality of forces outside their profession, to work with these forces in cooperative endeavors, and to
exert leadership in making the community a common foundation of
creative and critical thinking for the individual or group. At the least,
resource specialists are required by the objectives of their profession
to help the community define its information needs and work to establish
satisfactory communicative situations. Community organization is in-
tegrally related to the common content of problems, knowledge, objectives and methods which characterize communication science as a
whole.

Whenever in their daily lives people feel the need and impulse to
apply informed and deliberative direction to otherwise intuitive social
developments they make use of communication principles. Recorded
knowledge must have been collected and organized before they can expect a resource specialist to make it kinetic and relate it meaningfully
to the interests and concerns at hand. The interests and concerns within which the communicator makes knowledge kinetic are problems of
social structure, individual personality, and their interrelationships.
Such problems, of necessity, are identifiable, definable, and ultimately
solvable only in terms of particular forces and circumstances either
in the social environment or in people themselves. The central objective
of communication is to facilitate social adjustment through the development and constructive use of situations where the meaning of knowledge
and information can become kinetic in the lives of people.

Professional objectives are implemented when resource specialists in media, library, and information centers help individuals find
satisfying and fruitful relations in the social realities within which
they are involved. In addition, larger environmental arrangements
and relationships have to be adapted or modified for the satisfactory
social adjustment of all people in the community. This objective does
not seek to arbitrarily make over either the environment or the people
involved. On the contrary, a method is introduced and a process sustained whereby information is made meaningful to the problems of
social relationships and adjustments. Those involved in problems
are assisted in finding solutions satisfying to themselves and acceptable
to the society of which they are a part.

Communication service in media, library, and information centers
operates upon a faith in human beings, in their ability to educate themselves continuously and in their inherent right to choose and achieve
their own destiny through social relations of their own making within
a stable and progressive society. Resource communication has a deep
appreciation of individual differences and works for social progress
through the integration of these differences within the social fabric.
All communication service as well as the agency itself is tested by its
impact upon individual lives, and by its capacity to promote meaningful utilization of information for the individual and common good.

Resource service is a communicative, not a controlling function.
It is cooperative, not manipulative. A communication service is offered to those who need and want to make use of it in order to facilitate
adjustment, to foster constructive relationships, and to attain specific
individual ends. Resource communicators maintain a sensitive awareness of what happens to others who render information kinetic and meaningful in their lives. Even though the outcome rests with the information
user, the resource specialist's skill is consistently addressed to freeing
and enlisting an honest and responsive involvement in the communication
process.

The resource specialist seeks to facilitate the individual's contribution to the communicative experience by clarifying alternatives and
their consequences, by analyzing factors that enter into choice, and in
the evaluation and relation of the information elements to the individual's
objectives, available resources, and to the applications sought. The
core of the process is a disciplined use of oneself in direct relations
with people, and in a strategic as well as immediate and economical
exploitation of information sources wherever these need to located.

The resource communicator is a representative of a social agency which determines by its choice of purpose and policy the limits within which the professional operates.

The resource specialist as a representative of a social agency introduces into the development of individual and group purposes and relationships the stake of the larger community in the outcome and the basic social structure within which lesser relationships find a role. The resource agency represents the stable social whole within which individuals and groups find adjustment. The agency, based on a social contract, sustains and protects the professional in the helping, noncontrolling use of himself as a communicator, and exacts from his disciplined restraint in the use of his personal will and power. The resource agency conserves the basic democratic quality of noncontrolling communication as well as sustaining the essential framework of a stable and progressive society.

Community organization helps resource specialists accomplish their professional objectives, especially in their deliberately directed efforts to assist groups in attaining unity of purpose and action towards their general or specific objectives. Community organization facilitates social adjustment through the attainment of tangible and specific ends. Community organization is a long term method, not a goal, which resource centers share with all other agencies and organizations. The community is composed of powerful and often discontented forces that take a much longer time to become integrated than do those of individuals and face-to-face groups. Any community is the master of its own destiny. It may make mistakes but it also is a reservoir of insights and strengths which struggle to find outlet in the formulation and achievement of its democratic purposes.

Resource service to the community has traditionally been the broadest based program of all the agencies serving the community. There is no individual or group which does not have a claim to its informational and educational services. It is open to adults without regard to race, creed, color, or social standing. Its knowledge base is all encompassing. There is no boundary on the knowledge to which it has access and which it diffuses in order to bring about social change. The organized collection provides the basis upon which an interface can be established with the nonverbal and audiovisual message space of the people.

Resource service to the community exhibits all the characteristics of a coordinating structure that is so desperately needed in the disordered community endeavors of our time. Through community study and the identification of scarcely verbalized needs and interests as well as of community resources, professionals in the agency lay the basis for discharging its responsibility as a community clearinghouse. The center is in a stronger position than any other agency or organization for programming in the area of controversial issues (22). Finally the resource center has been delegated the responsibility to organize the groups which can promote evaluation and research in terms of community goals and objectives.

Various media exist as technological extensions of the media, library and information service programs and can be used to so saturate the awareness of the community as will make it difficult for citizens to avoid thinking about problems and concerns. In addition, electronic developments are currently available that can be used to bring resource services to people where they are located and not require them to travel to where the center happens to be situated. Such developments as the videophone and cablevision, when fully implemented, will probably make obsolete the proliferation of branch service outlets as they are known today and extend the present limited availability of service to a twenty-four hour, seven day-a-week basis.

Significant changes in the character of the population as to education, mobility and sophistication in the use of information services will increase the traditional librarians' defensiveness about scarcely warranted and almost totally uncoordinated types of library service. More people will expect to receive resource service at point of contact regardless of whether the service outlet may be administered by a public or any one of the special agencies. Cooperative activity among librarians of various types will of necessity increase as the burden of overlap, conflict of interest, and duplication of materials and services become increasingly onerous. The creation of an information utility may evolve that will be similar in nature to the electric telephone, or transportation utilities which now exist. This will increase the number of social choices or alternatives available to a wider portion of the community population.

With greater community involvement, groups of citizens will begin to give deeper attention to the significant issues of freedom of expression and freedom of assembly. Community involvement requires considerable motivation on the part of many people. There is probably no more effective way of engendering motivation than by programming in areas of controversial issues. Commitment to the identification of controversial issues will open up avenues of growth for professionals and citizens but dimly perceived in the traditional and superficially organized "freedom to read" campaigns organized for the defense of single proscribed titles. Freedom of assembly will become a way of life that will make it possible for more people in the community to become involved in decision making processes and release the energies of the power structure for more creative and cooperative endeavors.

As developments in the community increase and as additional resource services are expected, professionals and others will turn increasingly for understanding and for the development of coping abilities to the study of systems design and particularly social communications. The problems facing the community are becoming too complex to be easily solved by the addition of single uncoordinated facilities and services, and the supplying of "pre-packaged" programs not thoroughly related to group characteristics and interests. Various sources of income will have to be tapped and people in communities prepared for the partnership that will of necessity come among local, regional, and national tax appropriating bodies.

As traditional professionals move from the relatively easy problems of information transfer to those of meaning transfer, greater understanding of communication and learning theory will be required of them. If this occurs, various resource centers may yet return to the historical imperative of becoming a network of agencies dedicated solely to the continuing integrated learning of all citizens. But in order to do so priorities will have to be set and activities peripheral to this objective, such as the overemphasis upon service to children and youth, will have to be reappraised and, if necessary, abandoned.

In addition to these more obvious developments, there remain a few more or less minor concerns which exist in the nature of roadblocks or problems to be overcome. There is a general lack of awareness, especially among librarians, that a direct and immediate relationship exists between community development and a healthy democratic society. Unless people are involved over issues that concern them, community effort is taken for granted as a fine activity for "somebody else" but not to be taken seriously as a first order of business by library and other resource interests.

Few if any communities exist that are not "overorganized." But frequently what happens is that a small percentage of the population is "in everything" on a relatively superficial level. Concomitant with such superficial involvement is the great deal of organizational program time that is simply being filled to keep the membership of various community organizations from being too restive. Librarians aid and abet this situation in their reluctance to evaluate and challenge such pastime activity.

In our age of specialization it is easy for the professional to erect protective walls around himself and his agencies and to avoid areas that threaten "the security of the profession." But when fragmentation of effort and isolationism of interest occur it is not impossible to work also for the coordination and the interdependence so essential to the community leadership enterprise. Added to the growing sense of insecurity and inability to see the community whole is the general confusion about what resources to use in establishing priorities for productive community endeavor. There is a general futility even among professionals at the very size of the problems confronting the community and its often plethora of resource services.

But the challenge seems to be in recognizing the fact that long range self-interest of so many interests, apparently divergent, lies squarely in widespread community endeavor. To this self-recognition the professional can contribute, but the process becomes the easier to the extent that the resource specialist becomes sensitive and responsive to the actual and, more often than not, controversial needs and interests of all the people. Developments in the professional's own sensitivity and in his ability to apply the principles of communication will greatly accelerate a symbiotic relationship between the community and his agency.

THREE

COMMUNITY ORGANIZATION

This chapter presents a systems view of the community as a method which illustrates how a community is organized. It might be useful to discuss what is meant by a system and how such a view can be employed in examining the communication activities that are an integral part of any community. Although the term "system" has many definitions, a common one is that a system is a set of resources organized so that a set of goals can be accomplished.

A community can be thought of as a total system that is comprised of various subsystems. The subsystems are the components that represent objects, individuals, groups, institutions, organizations, and activities. A transportation system is an example of a subsystem component in a community system. There are five basic and minimal considerations to be kept in mind when thinking about a system (24):

Total system objectives or goals and, more specifically, the performance measures of the whole system

System's environment, or the fixed constraints

Resources of the system

Components of the system: their activities, goals, and measures of performance

Management of the system

The objectives of a community are sometimes stated in very general terms which make them almost useless as measures of performance. Frequently such objectives are really only implied and not stated at all. The implied objectives can be discovered by viewing the historical development of subsystems and their components as well as the lack of various subsystems and various subsystem components. Subsystems are developed to meet the objectives of a community and the lack of a subsystem reveals the lack of related objectives whether they are stated or not.

It is a very difficult task to separate the stated objectives from the real objectives. For example, the president of the school board will attempt to make us think that the sole objective of the educational system is the changing of pupil behavior when in reality the measure of performance is the grade. In another instance, the president of a trade union will tell us that the sole aim of his organization is to improve working conditions for the members while the actual measure of performance is the number of dues paying members. The real test of an objective of a system is the determination of whether the professional staff will knowingly sacrifice other goals in order to attain that objective. The point to observe is the consequent output of the system and not what the system says the consequences are or should be.

The environment of a system includes the things that lie outside the system. This is difficult to discern and the determination of an environment is subjective at best. From a systems viewpoint the environment of a community includes those activities, institutions, organizations, and people as well as their characteristics and behavior over which the community has relatively little control. These elements are the fixed or given constraints of the community system. For example, if certain state laws affect an urban community but cannot be changed by the community via any activity, then this legislation is an environmental constraint. The legislation is not only beyond the control of the community system, but determines partly how the community system performs.

DECISION COMPONENTS

Frequently, aspects of a community are thought to be outside community control when in fact they are not. Managers of the community have been known to use this excuse as a defense against criticism and poor performance on their part. An environmental constraint can be identified as a force which affects objectives but over which no control can be exerted. The pertinent questions to be posed about environmental constraints are:

Can anything be done about it?

Will the constraint hinder or stop the system from meeting a certain objective?

The resources of a community system are those things which are used to meet the objectives of the system. Resources are under control of the system and can be used to perform required tasks. The resources

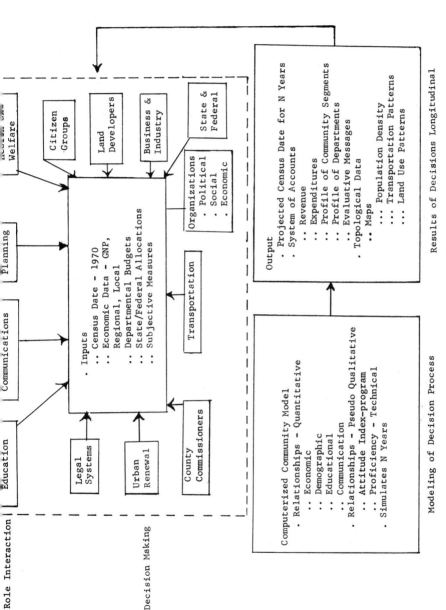

Figure 1 . Community Decision Components

are used to carry out the actions of the system. For example, a health
delivery subsystem may be composed of doctors, nurses, residents,
aides, orderlies, hospitals, clinics, first aid stations, rescue squads,
paramedics, pharmacies, pharmacists, medical supplies, salesmen,
etc. It is established, organized, regulated and managed to meet objectives related to health care. These objectives may not be written
down anywhere and may only exist in the expectations, demands, supports,
needs, and problems in the minds and actions of individuals or groups
in the community.

The health delivery subsystem and its components are resources
within the total community system. Of course, organizations, groups,
individuals as well as information, land, buildings, capital, products,
and machines are also resources of that system. The activities related
to each of the community resources are goal seeking in nature. Each
component's measure of performance is related to the measure of performance for the total community system. The difficulty occurs when
one tries to arrive at adequate measure of performance for the components and their activities. Various components have conflicting goals.
Therefore, overall system performance may be low while the performance
of individual subsystem components may be high but conflicting, thereby
offsetting each other.

The key to this problem is to determine what has been selected as
a measure of performance. Suppose the local school has accepted as
its measure of performance the lowest possible cost per pupil while
local business firms have established a performance measure that requires employing only "well educated people." It is possible that these
two performance measures will conflict to such an extent that the overall community systems measure of performance, to find employment
for all members, is seriously impaired. Conflict is not necessarily
bad in a social setting and more will be said about this later.

The managerial component of a system formulates the plans which
the system will follow. It also must ensure that such plans are implemented and followed in accordance with the control specifications. In
a community system the managers appear to be those elected and/or
appointed officials in the politicogovernmental subsystem. This however
is not always the case. The real managers sometimes hide behind the
scenes and manipulate the showcase managers like puppets. Normally
it takes some investigation in order to determine who the actual managers
are. In some cases the elected or appointed managers can share their
managerial position with others who have real power and have not become
completely dominated by them.

The necessity to receive information from the system and its environment requires that a system of communications be established which will provide for two way communication, both vertical and horizontal. The managers work to gather information from the community so that they can perceive the needs, problems, demands, supports, and expectations of the system being managed. This is normally referred to as feedback. When this feedback is used to make changes in the system, it is known as a cybernetic system.

In most communities only a "top-down" system is established and the managers are isolated from messages coming up from the lower level of the system or in from the external environment. This isolationism is a natural defense against an information or communication overload. This isolation is frequently imposed by the "Assistant to's," the Bureau Chiefs, and the staffers as a means to secure their own positions. It is important to realize that many systems of communication are established in a community. The managers have a communication system but so does every subsystem and component within the subsystems. In addition, visible and invisible communication networks evolve. There is considerable overlap in these networks and a single individual may belong to a dozen or more of them.

The managerial component tends to maintain a formal, visible communication network that is drawn along hierarchical lines. Such a management subsystem is usually called a bureaucracy. Hierarchy gives those at the top control of the formal communication system for a downward flow of messages. This permits the managers to manipulate those issues which can be raised as well as the solutions and decisions considered appropriate for community development. The managerial subsystems tend to overlap all other subsystems in the community. The further a subsystem is from the top of the hierarchical order the less authority it tends to have because it receives the fewest and most distorted messages.

The systems approach to community organization stresses that the relationships among component parts are as important as the parts themselves. Therefore, a community is viewed as relations not just things, contexts not just events, and interactions not statistics. The social scientist calls such an approach a collectivist approach. The difficulty of any approach to viewing a community is to distinguish between the macro and the micro level. The macro level is very compatible with the systems approach because it deals with supra units as opposed to smaller units such as family and individual. The smaller the unit the more difficult it is to define the relationships which exist because they tend to be invisible under layers and layers of higher level relationships. It may, of course, be possible to untangle the web of relationships on an individual level, but it seems more fruitful today to deal on a level above the individual because rugged individualism is quickly disappearing from the social scene.

The individual now uses the group, the organization or the institution as the way to mediate his needs, demands, expectations, and problems. The group, organization or institution in turn forms messages which are then placed in a communication channel that will hopefully carry the message to a higher level. If the message reaches the designated managerial level, a decision must be made as to how to deal with the message. Such decision making is important to the development of the community. The communication systems which exist are the only means that citizens in the community have for participating in the decision making process. Those who control the communication systems control knowledge and subsequently have the capacity to accumulate power. Thus the relationships that exist between systems components represent communication systems that have been designed or have simply grown out of necessity.

The utilization of such systems of communication to involve citizen groups in community development requires an understanding of how a community is organized as a system. An example of a systems view of a community might help to explain how a community functions and how the communication systems are organized. We must begin with some goals or objectives stated in rather simplistic terms. These might be:

To provide at least a twelfth grade education for every citizen

To provide a health delivery system that can serve every community member regardless of ability to pay for such services

To provide work opportunity for every citizen and a fair wage for work performed

To provide a community where crime is below national levels and it is safe to live

To allow citizens to accumulate power in proportion to
their ability or organize, bargain, employ strategy and
tactics, resolve conflicts or systemize information.

SYSTEM COMPONENTS

It may, of course, be nearly impossible to find a community where
such objectives are clearly stated or even stated at all. They usually
exist only as expectations in the minds of community members and have
been articulated for them by the communications elite. In any event,
each of the objectives stated above would tend to cause the creation of
a subsystem in the total community system. Thus the five objectives
stated above might cause the establishment of the following subsystems
respectively:

Educational System
Public Health System
Economic System
Crime and Safety System
Political Power System

Each of these subsystems can be extremely complex and difficult
to understand. In fact, each of them can be further subdivided into
sub-subsystems. But all these subsystems and their sub-subsystems
are not separable from each other or the community as a whole. This
orientation is the key to a systems view and analysis of a community.
All the systems and subsystems are held together by relationships which
exist between them. Communication systems are established along
these relationships. The type of relationship may be dependent, cooperative, parasitic, dominant, or symbiotic. The basis of the relationship may be power, economic, psychological, social, or cultural.

Unfortunately, these relationships and the nonseparability of such
subsystems only become visible during a crisis. Let us suppose that
the school system as one component of the educational system of a community has been closed by a teachers' strike. An immediate result is
that women who work must consider remaining at home to care for the
children. They may have to find and hire someone else to care for their
children, or else allow the children to stay home by themselves. In
the first two cases, this represents a loss of income. In some families
such a loss will mean having to give up essential services or items
which may be necessary for their well-being. If necessary medical
services have to be given up, this decision may at a later date cause

an emergency situation with which the health delivery system will have
to deal. In extreme cases, where the disrupted work pattern is the only
source of income, the welfare system will be affected by adding people
to its rolls.

The economic system is disturbed in many other ways. The loss
of income to those on strike and those affected by the strike reduces
their purchasing power and local retailers may feel the pinch. Banks,
savings and loan institutions, and others in the financial subsystem find
their capital flowing out to meet emergencies. This unproductive trend
begins to influence their investment capabilities and their relationships
with the external environment. In some extreme cases those who are
in need of money and goods taken away by the strike may revert to il-
legal means to get assistance. Recourse to criminal methods increases
the load on the crime and safety system. Or again because an increased
number of children are now on the streets or in parks and other areas
for entertainment purposes, the safety system is again involved in addition to the parks and recreation systems. Libraries and other information systems are also utilized more for entertainment, educational,
and informational purposes.

If the strike is not settled quickly, the educational goals of the community are seriously threatened. In many communities the absence of
children attending schools affects certain economic relationships with
the environment such as state and federal funds based on school attendance. Various volunteer components in the total social services system
may be affected because all of the available volunteers are now tending
children at home. The legal system becomes involved with various systems in addition to the crime and safety system. It will be required to
negotiate the strike itself as well as bring suits against, and hear cases
concerning various parties involved in the strike. It may also have to
hand down decisions on behalf of citizens' and other community organizations.

The managerial subsystem will be involved in attempting to mediate
the strike or in demanding its termination. Eventually the power system
and political system may be brought in to settle the matter. In fact, if
the strike cannot be settled there is a danger that the community leaders
concerned may lose their political or power positions. One could go on
to show how the utility system, the sanitary system, the transportation
system, and others can be affected by a disruption to the educational
system. It is sufficient to say that all the community systems are related in some manner and to some degree. It is only the type and degree

of the relationship which causes one community to function differently from another. Although in reality one cannot separate one system from another it is sometimes desirable to do so in order to model, analyze, and discuss it in detail without being confused by all the complex interrelationships. The important thing to remember under such circumstances is the assumptions underlying the model when you strip away reality.

The importance of viewing a community as a system is that if forces one to consider relationships in addition to patterns, structures, and characteristics. This view of the community develops an appreciation of the subsystems in the community as communication sources and channels which transmit messages to other subsystems and their components. It is assumed that all subsystems which make up a community comprise a complex communications system composed of a sophisticated network that expands and contracts as societal needs, demands, expectations, supports, and goals expand, contract, and change. The nonverbal actions of the police as well as the verbal messages they communicate to other system components in the community illustrate the expectations they have and how they have interpreted messages from the community. In turn, the police receive messages from various subsystems such as labor, business, industry, adolescents, elderly, young adults, wealthy, poor, blacks, orientals, criminals, managers.

Any list of subsystems will include many overlapping components such as the citizens who are both black and young adults. Young adults, for example, can be considered as a subsystem composed of the components, black young adults. These components constitute a system because as a group of people young adults have goals they desire to achieve and relationships that they have established that enable them to achieve their goals. The system of young adults contains numerous components some of which are subgroups of people such as black young adults, poor young adults, poor black young adults, wealthy black young adults. Being young adults they have many common goals and problems which cause them to be related in many ways to each other and to other systems.

The police may communicate to young adults their concern about the safety of young children. This concern might be in response to messages they have received from the total system of citizens. The police may at the same time establish communication with young adult groups over the "message" that payday "hell" raising will not be tolerated and that they will use whatever force is necessary to deal with this problem. This transmission may be done without spoken words being passed between the police and young adults. Nonverbal actions and informal net-

works can and do operate as powerful media of communication within
any community. On the other hand when it becomes quite obvious that
the messages being sent by the police are not congruent with community
goals, the community system will send very strong messages informing
the police that they must realign themselves with the efforts of the community as a whole.

LEVELS OF ANALYSIS

It may seem that the concept of a system has been limited to a
group of people. But it is also common to speak of a system of abstract
entities such as ideas. Much of science is thought of as a system of
ideas, theories, and facts. An important element in viewing a community as a system without becoming bogged down in detail is to select the
level at which it is desirable to analyze the community. This will depend
on the purpose for which community analysis is being done.

A complete macrosystems view of a community would deal only with
the top level relationships of large systems such as the managerial sys-
tem, economic system, educational system, social service system, information system, and the physical system. This structure usually turns
out to be a formal system as illustrated in Figure 2: Hierarchical
Authority Relationships. Such an analysis of community structure and
relationships is useful only for the most superficial generalizations about
a community. This initial analysis describes only the formally recognized and major channels of communication. It is necessary to have
additional analyses done for every other network of relationships. It
then becomes interesting to consider where the various subsystems can
be located within the community as well as the sociodramatic interplay
of community transactions.

Various methods of analyzing communication systems and techniques
can be useful in determining the relationships that exist in a community,
even though at best most relationships have so far only been determined
in a subjective manner for community systems. The usual method of
showing how a community is structured and functions is to gather statistical data on the various systems that exist. This will normally include data on the physical system (acres of land, blocks, streets,
buildings, space utilization, topology), the educational system (number
of students by grade, race, reading level), the economic system (community income, expenditures, types of businesses and industries, tax
base, skilled and unskilled labor by race, type).

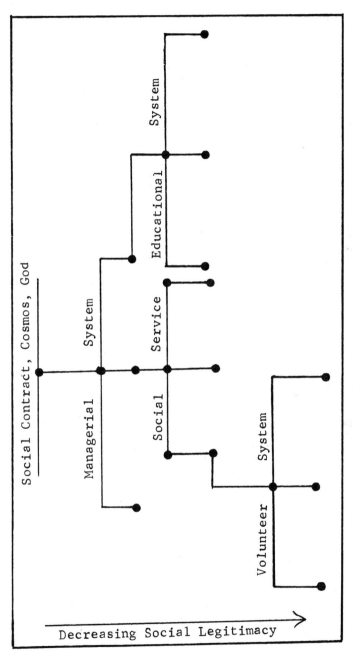

Figure 2 . Hierarchical Authority Relationships

Unfortunately, few attempts have been made to go beyond such descriptive data however initially important it may be. But to discover the true nature of a community requires that one go beyond the census and serial survey. What is needed in addition to the descriptive data is data on the relationships which exist between systems. Each subsystem must be considered from the sociocultural, economic transactional, and dramatic nature of its intersystem relationships. One must begin to uncover the networks that hold a community together and describe the relationships as precisely as possible at the required level of detail between nodes in a single network and between two or more networks.

An objective such as this requires a prolonged observation of each network to find out the channels along which flow orders, instructions, requests, advice. The frequency, nature, intention, content, and causes or effects of such messages must be utilized to arrive at a definition of the relationships that exist. It must be remembered that one is not dealing with the life history of a single individual but with averages, rates and probabilities. The economic system deals with averages and aggregates such as average incomes, investment rates, prices, taxation. An individual may provide the link between one system and another and in that case the individual represents a relationship rather than an entity.

COMMUNITY STRUCTURES

The generally accepted notion used to define a community is a physical or politically bounded area that offers a link between individuals and the totality of society. However, such a use of physical and political boundaries has been found to be inadequate in the sense that more than one community may exist within a designated physical or political boundary. This can be seen in large urban areas wherein there may exist dozens of communities. Individuals identify with the east side, or the west side or some other community in any large urban area. Individuals live in a system of systems or organizations that are related in such a way that through their interactions the individual's needs, demands, and expectations are served.

A community involves a sense of belonging or feeling over and above any artificial or natural boundaries which may exist. Community involves people joining together to achieve certain goals. These goals incorporate the major social functions which have some relevance to the maintenance of the social systems that exist. This includes those activities which afford people access to community systems necessary for day to day living. The community as an area of common activity and interest is composed of institutions, organizations, and informal groups which are interdependent in the total system of community life (33):

Community institutions include schools, churches, welfare agencies, business, and industry which perform well defined and necessary functions. Because of their fixed areas of responsibility, bureaucratic organization, and established patterns of operation, institutions make slow adjustments to changing conditions and then only when forced to by public demand. Institutions may also serve as focal points around which organizations known as satellite groups can be formed.

Formal associations include the multiplicity of clubs, lodges, church societies, fraternities, and professional associations. This associational structure overlaps and interacts with institutions as well as with the informal groups. Formal associations are themselves engaged in community education and action. They usually have sufficient flexibility to meet change and new needs if their purposes are broad enough to permit active commitment to community action.

Informal groups include the unstable and various patterns of social interaction which eddy around the institutional and organizational structure of the community. These groups or "talking chains" often lack well-defined structure and are difficult to involve in organized community activities. They are sometimes moved to action by confrontation tactics and activists groups.

Despite these structures, there is usually a substantially large segment of the population which remains to be reached through means other than organized groups. One approach is to identify and work through informal groups. Informal groups are more difficult to identify. They are spontaneously formed and seldom have established relations with institutional programs. The communicator may find that his best approach for reaching and involving these informal groups is to identify their leaders, try to get them interested, and capitalize on their influence in involving the group as a whole.

A community adhesive function is performed when associations help institutions and communities to adjust to each other. Institutions use their systems of satellite clubs to supplement, augment, and support

their programs. Satellites operate as pseudo-primary groups to human-
ize the institutions in the eyes of the community as a whole. Churches
and many economic organizations surround themselves with associations
which helps to dissolve the antagonisms felt by the community towards
them.

Associations operate as communications links in the chain of authority between top community leadership and the community at large. Cultural, religious, and veterans organizations appear to be involved only
slightly in this process while civic clubs, business, and professional
groups are more heavily involved. There are other chains of communication, however, which have potential significance. When an institution
cosponsors an activity with an association it uses the association's link
to its membership. The increased use of such associational networks
is a very effective means of establishing two-way communication with
significant segments of the community and of increasing the range of
community participation.

A community can be a concrete and living experience which is discovered by people who need a sense of security and belonging. Geographic and political boundaries are important, not literally, but in the sense
of their influence on people and their needs. It is important to realize
that the community is a social unit defined by the behavior patterns of
people. The concept of community exists on various levels with various
degrees of meaning. Community in the United States can mean the entire nation, a state, a county, a city, a township, or a ward. Those
activities and feelings which make the state a community on one level
and the city on another are a matter of type and degree. It is analogous
to the relationship an individual may feel he has with the local union
and the one he has with the national organization.

A community, then, is the image of many expectations and represent-
ations in the minds of people. It is as much a matter of common feeling
and identification as it is a matter of material and physical components.
The relationships and transactions identify a group of people who share
a number of common interests and participation in a common life style
whether on some forced or freely acceptable level. Sanders (121) has
identified some of these objectives which hold a community together:

Community loyalty might be compared to patriotism at the
national level or morale in the armed forces. Community
loyalty is usually stronger in those communities which
are democratically organized and operated. It is strong

in communities in which people know what is going on and why. Loyalty also involves change. People do not fear or resist change when they understand the necessity for it. One measure of community morale is the extent to which the people accept and help direct desirable changes in the community.

Leaders must see, understand, and work for the whole community. Every community has some type or kind of leadership. Every normal individual has leadership capabilities under certain conditions. However, many leaders are special interest leaders who see only one segment of community life, such as the school, or the church, or the civic club. But their leadership capabilities can be further developed in order to work for the community as a whole.

Institutions serve the community and it is as strong or as weak as are these institutions. Institutions must be interlocked or intermeshed so that all of them support a common set of basic values. If for example, one makes the unfortunate mistake of suggesting that certain laws need not be obeyed, then all governmental functioning in the community, state, and nation is weakened. The underlying values become less important, and in the functioning of other institutions the family is weaker, the church is weaker, the school is weaker.

Economic stability and growth are basic factors in building a good community. Sound community life must be based on job opportunities, adequate payrolls, with industry diversified enough to cushion the community from the ups and downs of the business cycles. These economies must be integrated so as to produce a higher level of living for all people.

Problem solving in a collective way is essential to a healthy community life. Since problems exist largely in the minds of people, the citizens should be involved in as wide a range of decision making as possible.

The above characteristics are dependent upon an adequate and well developed system of communication in a community. This system of

communication allows the citizen to participate in the improvement and
development of his physical and social environment. For example, a
ghetto dweller may feel that the ghetto is his community because that
is where he is a part of the decision-making, power, and social structure
on a very involved level. It gives the citizen a feeling that he has a
part in the decision making and power structure of his community, and
that certain social functions necessary to his survival are performed
by and through his community. The more involvement the citizen feels
with the decision making and social functions which maintain him, the
stronger will the feeling be of community and of the values obtained
which have been identified by Lindeman (83):

> Working to create a better life for all citizens can be a
> satisfying and fulfilling experience.

> Differences can be resolved in the lab of community life
> through broad selfeducational efforts.

> Democratic aims and methods can be experienced when-
> ever cooperative enterprises are developed.

> National and world problems can be appraised to better
> advantage and dealt with more realistically in the local
> community.

> Character and personality can be built in local community
> endeavors as contacts with neighbors supplement home
> influences.

> Public opinion formed in interpersonal transactions
> becomes a more reliable guide to and arbiter of the
> community mores.

> Self-reliance is engendered in the citizens and the lead-
> ership when outside resources (government, foundations)
> are employed productively rather than passively accepting
> such services as handouts.

The city within which the individual exists is of course a community,
but it is often a community on a more remote and abstract level than
the neighborhood. By the same token, the state is also a community.
However, the more involved the individual is and the greater the opportunity he has to control his life style, the greater the feeling of community.

A president probably thinks of the entire United States as his community because of the degree of control he has in that context whereas a governor will tend to think in terms of his state as a community. On the other hand, the context can be reduced to a micro situation where an individual feels his only community is the house or apartment he lives in.

CHANNELS OF COMMUNICATION

Citizens need some means for participating in activities and decisions which control and otherwise affect their lives in order to help them deepen and widen their feeling of community involvement. The opening up of existing channels of communication and developing new channels where necessary is of the utmost importance in community development. A community is a dynamic living organism which is composed of numerous systems and components that contract, expand and develop so that it is adaptable to the social needs of the people who live there. It is felt by some that the social organization called a community is uncontrollable and takes a shape or design that allows the system to exploit individuals. But this view can only be held if one also holds the view of rugged individualism which is an outdated and unrealistic view in a complex modern society.

A more viable view of the community is that of a system composed of a set of interlocking subsystems within which there exist conflict and tension. Neither a dictatorial or consensus mode of decision making considers and utilizes conflict. Multiple models employed to represent a problem or process are particularly useful when arriving at a decision. The structure, composition, and interrelationships which exist within the community act as an environment. These constraints may influence the manner in which individuals behave. But they may at the same time serve as channels for individuals to control the environment by communicating their needs, expectations, problems, demands, and supports via the channels available or constructed by those who can make the necessary response. In some cases this may mean communicating to an individual, a group of individuals, an organization, an entire system, all the systems or the entire membership of the community.

Communication only takes place if the message that is sent reaches the required destination and the message received has the same meaning for the sender(s) and the receiver(s). Messages are intended to influence the receiver but they may not always be spoken or written. Sometimes they are simply nonverbal events which contain a great deal of information. Such actions are powerful messages and usually evoke a response although not always of a desirable type (88).

In any community with multiple systems, there will exist conflicting goals and conflicts over how to reach the same goal. The test of how well the managers of the community can manage can be determined by how well they make use of conflict. Conflict as opposed to consensus is a powerful tool for solving social problems. Conflict will bring out the important aspects of a problem that usually never get looked at when using a consensus mode of decision making. Conflict resolution allows inputs from all those who believe that they have an aspect of the problem which has been overlooked or a solution that has not been considered.

Conflict resolution creates a situation within which a considerable amount of data and solutions can be presented. It is then the job of the decision maker to synthesize the data and solutions and eventually make the best decision possible. This mode of operation allows the various subsystems and individual components to become informed about the various alternatives and conflicts over goals, solutions, and resource allocations. Such a method tends to create a feeling of community because the citizen has feedback from his opinion, data, or solution for consideration and feels he has been a part of the decisions being made which affect his life.

The size of a community has an affect on its systematic organization and functions. As a community grows larger, there is a need for more complex systems. As a result, systems such as politics, economics, religion, and social service change in structure and function. When the community reaches a size where a segment of the population feels it is not dependent upon the rest of the system, a new community forms and thus a cell division type of process begins. As a community grows so does the need for specialization. This can be vividly seen in a very small community where one man may act as the mayor, judge, tax collector, and minister. As the community increases in size one man cannot assume all these jobs and a division of labor occurs with specialists needed to perform each job.

In addition, as the density of a community grows and as it increases so does competition, aggrandizement, and exploitation. This expansion of vested interest tends to cause disorder and the need for more formal controls is demanded. Increased control results in more sophisticated systems and complex interrelations between systems. Greater complexity requires more coordination between systems such as the system of service agencies, the system of volunteer agencies, the legal system, the law enforcement system, the political system, the system of social groups, and the economic system. Coordination is necessary because the increase in system components creates a sense of disorder which needs to be reduced for the members of the community.

Some reduction in disorder can be affected by combining those systems performing similar functions and by defining for community members the roles and functions of various subsystems. Once components and interrelationships have been identified, referral routes can be established so that people can follow up on their problems and potential problems. This type of coordination allows the individual members of the community to better understand their roles as well as the roles of the numerous subsystems, their components and interrelationships. It is the interrelationships among the various subsystems which is so important to identify and establish in order to serve the needs of the community and its members. Interrelationships are often referred to as vertical and horizontal ties. The horizontal lines refer to relationships between subsystems in the community whereas the vertical ties refer to relationships outside the system.

The local system of labor unions has vertical ties with national unions' headquarters in other communities and the local General Electric plant has vertical ties to its out-of-community headquarters. These vertical ties can have as profound an effect on a community as the horizontal ones. A decision by GE headquarters to close its local plant can have a major affect on all the other community systems. On the other hand, the vertical ties allow many new ideas, customs, and usages to flow in from the larger society. In any event, the power system in a community is frequently established along the lines of those who have the vertical ties to the outside. Consequently, most forms of local community control are ineffective when applied to the vertical relationships even though they may be quite effective for the horizontal relationships.

A community is a system of systems that includes numerous formal and informal subsystems that grow up within a community. A community is not centralized in structure and function in the same sense as a formal organization. A community is a social system whose definition includes the behavior of individuals who live there and is as much a feeling as it is the goal seeking behaviors that can be identified. Thus the processes that take place in a community are as important as the content.

Although every community differs to some extent in degree and type, there are certain systems that exist for the maintenance of daily

living. The physical system includes the material characteristics of
the space in which the community is located. This includes elements
such as access routes via land, air, and water; kind and condition of
buildings; kinds of flora and fauna; climatic and subsoil conditions.
While the physical system places boundary conditions on the other systems in the community, the study of human geography or urban geography
is a fast developing and fruitful area of investigation for community
development.

The economic system is concerned with the production, distribution
and consumption of wealth. It provides the material means necessary
to maintain the daily life of the members of a community. This system
includes the sources of revenue as well as the expenditure and the development of resources both human and physical in order to satisfy human
needs. Within this system various other subsystems can be considered
such as the retail products business system, the service business system, the production industries, the labor system and the financial system.
Within the economic subsystem exchanges are made between the components. Time and skills are exchanged as a medium of barter, and goods
are produced.

The component of labor which has been considered as a subsystem
of the economic system could just as well be thought of as a macrosystem
within which the economic system is embedded. In any event these two
systems are closely related. The labor system is composed of those
individuals and groups who have certain skills, time, and energy to
offer which can be utilized in order to provide goods or services for
themselves and others in the community and outside the community. In
many communities the laboring force is organized to ensure adequate
wages and working conditions.

The health system includes those institutions, individuals, and groups
of individuals who are responsible for caring for others in the community
who contact a disease or are injured. The sanitary system is very closely
related to the health system. In some cases these same components belong to the safety system which attempts to protect people against disease
and injury. The safety system is responsible for protecting the community from physical danger such as fire, crime, injury, and disease. Normally the fire, police, and public health departments are a part of this
system. Of course, the entire health system is closely related to the
safety system as well as citizen groups and private enterprise with a
social conscience.

The educational system is responsible for producing individuals with the skills and competencies needed in order to join the labor force or other community systems as well as provide the community with a future via its educated members. The objective of the educational enterprise is to teach students the cultural and value objectives of the community. It is also important to recognize that it is largely within the educational system that social groups become known to and established for each new generation.

Not all the graduates of the educational system can be absorbed by the economic system and not all who could be absorbed desire to be. Consequently, a system of welfare is usually established to take care of these and other people. This system could have the very simple objective of not charging for goods and services. More often welfare is a complex system of support by outside agencies using payments of money, reduced fees for services, free housing, food stamps, social security, pensions, etc.

Since adequate housing is a major problem in many urban areas, systems of housing, land development, and renewal are usually evident. The housing system contains as components the landlords, tenants, housing codes, the public health and safety systems, the economic system, and parts of many other subsystems. Its main purpose is to provide adequate housing for all members of the community. Unfortunately, the housing system is often in perpetual conflict with many of its components and many other systems. As a result this system is in a constant state of change and in need of improvement.

The public works system which includes public access pathway maintenance and development becomes involved in the transportation system to a great extent as well as the safety system. In most areas urban transportation is a critical problem. The purpose of the transportation system is to move people and goods from one location to another as quickly, economically, and safely as possible. Components include all modes of transportation such as plane, bus, taxi, private car, truck, train, subway and boat. Since the problems of this system have been critical in large urban areas, the lack of adequate transportation has caused fundamental changes in many of the other systems in the community.

The public utilities system overlaps many other systems and is responsible for the supplying and regulating of electrical service, gas service, and communication services to the members of the community.

This system has close relationships with many other components in the community such as the economic system, the housing system, the communication, and information systems. The regulation of utilities as well as other subsystems in the community is a function of decision making which in turn is involved with the managerial system, the power and influence system, the political system, the judicial system, the communication, and information system as well as the social status system.

From the foregoing it may seem that most communities are heavily overorganized and systemized. But despite the appearances of systemization which may exist, there are large segments of most communities that are involved only in a peripheral manner with the decision making processes. The methods, content, and development of programs are all too often limited by the patterns of local resources both physical and human. Talking chains must be started so that it is difficult for people to avoid thinking about fundamental issues and, hopefully, begin to participate in information-gathering and educational experiences associated with those fundamental issues.

The community coordinating structure should seek to support and strengthen the existing organizations in the community. At no time must there develop a feeling of competition between it and any special interest group in the community. In fact, one of the major purposes is to arouse participation in special interest groups and to develop effective leaders not only for their own organizations but for all other organizations in the community. Communitywide development provides one sure way in which people can come together to think, plan, and act. It involves the individual members of the community in surveying community needs and in creating community support as a prelude to community action.

Community development can be defined as something people do when they try to balance their community needs with their community resources. It operates against the small, well organized group that, convinced of the righteousness of its own cause, presumes to speak for all citizens. It provides opportunities for the most humble citizen to be a participant in making things happen in accordance with his own needs and wishes. In return for the effort organization requires, the individuals concerned hope to create for themselves and their neighbors a better community in which to earn a living and raise a family.

FOUR

COMMUNITY CHANGE AGENT

The role of a community change agent has been developed within
the profession of media, library, and information science. This role
can be best realized when the change agent is not employed by an institution or agency of government. The communicator is employed by
his client groups as an advocate or ombudsman. He may serve his clients
as an individual or as a member of a professional team who are self-
employed.

The resource communicator is a change agent by virtue of his ability
to recognize as well as create situations wherein information surprises
can occur, and not simply by virtue of the fact that he may be the manager
or staff member of a service infrastructure. The knowledges, attitudes
and skills to be attained are those required of an ombudsman and an advocate. These may include the ability to organize information space as
well as retrieval skills, but of greater significance is an information-
surprise "sense" with which he can create provocative and developmental
contexts so that the patron whether individual or group can work for his
own maturity.

Considerable innovation has occured with a number of models
and methods that have been employed in order to redeploy the infrastructure of media, library, and information science. It is one thing to pur-
sue the objective of coordinating the informational and educational services of the community. It is quite another to undertake advocacy services and claim the role of ombudsman, or attempt to coordinate the
various advocacy services available to the citizen. But it is being undertaken because the sociocultural and information space continuously being
created by the symbol manipulators needs to be mediated by a helping
profession.

The mass media are effective in arousing attention, but it remains
for the communications change agent to so mediate the community that
citizens can satisfy their stimulus hunger and relate information surprise to their everyday concerns and interests. The communications
elite as symbol manipulators in a free enterprise system more often
serve economic and propagandistic purposes than educational and

Even the informal groups, members rank themselves depending upon the extent to which they represent or are able to realize the values of the group. There is a built-in psychological reward for participants who go along with the group. For those who deviate, the group process temporarily suspends discussion and persuasion in order to bring them into line, employing disapproval and lowered ranking and finally outright expulsion. Those expelled may form their own group with different criteria for membership and standards for ranking. Those who cannot find acceptance within the so-called socially legitimate groups may require the advocacy of floating librarians in order to avoid the borderline groupings of illegitimacy, delinquency or crime.

In any event, every person needs not only group encounter, but effective counseling for group participation. The professional advocate must have an informed sense of social issues and an understanding of the conditions within which individuals encounter one another and form into developmental groups. Persons concerned about acceptance and with a need for recognition and for stabilizing their interpersonal perceptions may yet find themselves outside the established channels of custom, or law or the prevailing arrangements of social organizations. In such instances, these individuals will tend to interact among themselves.

Repeated group interaction leads to the differentiation of roles and functions which help the collective to meet its goals whatever these may be. The norms established and maintained become aspects of each participants conscience. The advocate must be able to anticipate or help to shape the process of structure and norm development within various groups. Both the environmental setting and the information space become of increasing importance for the behavioral alternatives encouraged or permitted as the social collective moves from informal perception to choate awareness and technological change.

Disruptive tactics are frequently used for revolutionary change and presuppose some system of choice. Disruptive tactics are preceded by a choice made on the basis of moral and ethical considerations before strategic objectives are identified and sought. Whatever the actual social reality may be, different perceptions of what change should be sought by each party in an encounter situation are significant in determining their responses (146). Strategy requires a long-term plan of action which is based on some theory of communication; while tactics are the more recurrent methods of action. A strategy for change might utilize tactics from one or more modes of intervention simultaneously,

munications "elite" is a self-selected group of comparatively few individuals who by their communicative efforts move a community or a society
from an informal to a formal awareness of fundamental social issues.

INFORMAL TO FORMAL AWARENESS

The time lag between the creation of new knowledge by the disciplines and such formal awareness of it as will influence social policy
can only be reduced by effective professional and socially relevant leadership. Leadership is a function of the ability of an individual(s) to per-
sonify group norms. Intellectual leadership provides initiative, guidance,
new ideas, and proposals for solutions. Social leadership, on the other
hand, engenders mutual acceptance, liking, harmony, and congeniality.
In most groups intellectual leadership is deemphasized in favor of the
popular role. Most participants will choose to be liked the best rather
than to have the best ideas. Leadership consequently may be considered
to be a function of motivation, expectation of success and incentive for
accomplishment.

Active social participation is essential for professional leadership
because it is more effective to influence people as group members than
as isolated individuals. The people's perception of social issues moves
from informal to choate awareness as social participants are motivated
to change in the direction in which control (leadership or influence) has
been validated by consensus. The greater the number of individuals who
participate, the more important the issue becomes for the group and the
surer the collective is about what the criteria are for true or correct
behavior. Group instability occurs when the standards external to the
group become indefinite or are the product of one strong-willed source.
The group process tends to set standards for a whole range of individual
behavior, not simply for those activities which come within the jurisdiction of any single group by itself.

Perceptions occur and awareness is strengthened because the group
provides rewards for proper behavior and punishment for improper behavior. The rewards are support, reinforcement, security, morale,
encouragement, protections, and, especially, rationale as distinct from
rationalization. The punishments may include ridicule, dislike, shame,
and the threat of expulsion. These rewards and punishments may sound
intangible but they are extremely effective (37). "Such values are not
material, like money, but are often more valuable — not only from the
larger community in the form of fame, but within the intimate personal
group in the form of love" (100).

ones. Nevertheless, these communications leaders do create the socio-cultural networks of sign and symbol so necessary to the effective develop-ment and maintenance of social relationships.

A sociocultural information space of this nature is a pervasive en-vironmental factor of considerable significance in helping people move from an informal to a formal awareness of social issues. A commun-ications change agent serves a primary social purpose by ensuring that this "running" sociocultural commentary becomes a cognitive-affective map to which the average citizen can relate his everyday disparate ex-periences and thereby find meaning for them. He also needs to become aware of the role of technology in society and of his own responsibility for its development whether he is passively or actively involved.

The communications change agent has historical antecedents in the resource profession and the appearance of the role can be located within the community development enterprise (117). Since the beginning of the public library movement in America, many librarians have emphasized community development (76). But more often than not, the role of such community agents has been narrowly conceived (103) as largely doing public relations for the infrastructure of media, library, and information science. The younger members of the profession have turned the com-munity worker concept into a people oriented professional role and re-named it the "floating" librarian (108).

At a time when institutions, agencies and organizations struggle to establish a "relevant" interface between themselves and the community, the role of the change agent or floating librarian is of considerable im-portance to the leaders of media, library, and information professions. This is particularly significant today when the function of the satellite group, whose purpose was to cushion and interpret the impact of an agency upon the community, is being seriously challenged by concerned citizens on all socioeconomic and cultural levels (2). One has but to re-view the literature (32) of "friends of libraries" (118) to realize how little relevance this one type of satellite group has for a wide range of concerns and interests of actual people living in the contemporary ur-ban community.

The role of the community resource specialist has emerged in the profession as the coalescence of several and often disparately perceived developments. In essence, however, the floating librarian functions as a communications leader (107) whose role has been explicated if not de-fined albeit in a formal way by Hall (54). According to Hall, the com-

depending upon the goals of the action system and the organizational context within which it operates (99) (see Table 1: Strategies of Organized Behavior).

The process of group formation is of concern to any profession but especially to those with an advocacy role to fulfill. Group formation depends to a considerable degree upon the nonverbal and audiovisual message space and facilities of the environment as well as the relation of one group to others whose activities and aims impinge favorably or unfavoaraly upon those of the group in formation (126). There are four essentials in the process of group formation: repeated interaction growing out of a common motivational base; structured (organization) development consisting of roles and statuses; formation of rules, traditions, values, and norms; differential attitude and behavior development among participants over time.

Even the mere social presence of other persons has some effect on behavior and task performance which over time begin to assume regularities. Sherif (127) indicates three objective ways by which norm development and regularity can be detected in the group and organizational enterprise of any community:

By observing similarities and regularities in the behaviors (word and deeds) found among one set of persons but not another set in a similar situation.

By observing correctives (sanctions) for certain behaviors and praise or reward for others. Reactions to deviations are among the best evidence of the bounds of acceptable behavior. These may range from disapproval, frowns and correctives to threats and actual punishment.

By noting the increasing similarity or convergence over time in the behaviors of individuals who initially behaved differently. For example, the entrance of a new member into a group provides an opportunity to detect the existence of its norms.

Communication bears an organic relation to society (101). It is not separate from the rest of society. It is really the interpersonal intersections of society and varies by function more in degree than in kind. Communications, whether in a modern state or a traditional one, is the enterprise which handles the cognitive and affective business of society.

Table 1. Strategies of Organized Behavior

If change is:	Then response is:	And intervention is:	And tactic is:
Rearrangement of resources	Consensus	Collaborative	Joint action Cooperation Education
Redistribution of resources	Difference	Campaign	Comprise Arbitration Negotiation Bargaining Mild Coercion
Change in status relationships	Dissensus	Contest or disruption	Clash of position within accepted social norms Violation of normative behavior (manners) Violation of legal norms
Reconstruction of entire system	Insurrection	Violence	Deliberate Attempts to harm Guerilla warfare Deliberate attempt to take over government by force

It passes back and forth the danger signals over how to satisfy needs as
well as the decision signals by which any organism tries to maximize
its desired functioning. In the process, the organism works to minimize
the associated stress and strain and maintain a satisfactory working
balance between it and society (see Figure 3: Community Interactive
Behaviors).

At any moment in the history of society the function of a communicative profession (34) is to do whatever is required by society. It is
one thing to claim the role of a communications profession and thus
perhaps obtain a reputation for leadership, but quite another to perform
as a communications leader as Hall has considered the function or as
Stone (133) envisioned the role of the community change agent many years
ago. Considerable research has been undertaken on the role of the community change agent in extending the influence of mass communication
(68). Opinion leaders not only influence the content and viewpoints expressed in the mass media, but through organizations and other reference groups, deepen that influence (70). In addition, earned leadership
within the neighborhoods continues to propel these and other influences
down through the talking chains to the average citizen.

Community development (115) is the social method used by society
to help people develop the material well-being of all citizens. It is also
used as a means of preserving or developing and enhancing the effectiveness of democratic processes and principles. Community development may employ either or both of two general methods to meet the interests and solve problems in the sociopolitical collective. On the one
hand, a market decision can be made in which all of the individuals involved decide on the course of action to be taken. In order to do this,
for example, without collective organization and planning, the decision
is made on the basis of numerous (perhaps thousands) of independent
votes recorded in a poll (49). On the other hand, administered decisions
can be made by a few individuals in an institutional or political infrastructure. These individuals are supposed to be representatives of and
empowered to act for the collective through some form of delegated
authority. Leadership of a type may be involved in the administered
decision despite the fact that it may be difficult to describe it as communicative leadership.

The infrastructure out of which the communications change agent
operates reflects the structure and development of society (145). The
size of the communications enterprise reflects the economic development of society. Communications activity includes the mass media and

POTENTIAL CONFLICT

Conflict = Two or more groups competing for limited resources, power positions, prestige etc, resisting change or the threat of change.

▼ High
O Med
X Low

Direction of Interaction

1 State Administrator
2 Federal Administrator
3 State Librarian
4 Fed. Div. of Libraries
5 County Manager
6 County Planner
7 County Communications
8 Urban Renewal
9 Anti Poverty (CAP)
10 HEW
11 Land Developer
12 Citizens
13 Communications Budget
14 "   Planner
15 "   Agents
16 Conventional Librarians
17 County Council
18 Council of Librarians
19 Tax Association
20 Business and Industry

Column headings (targets):

1 State
2 Federal
3 State Lib.
4 Fed. Div. of Lib.
5 Manager
6 Planner
7 Communications
8 Renewal
9 Poverty (CAP)
10 HEW
11 Land Dev.
12 Citizens
13 Comm. Budget
14 Planner "
15 Agents "
16 Conv. Lib.
17 County Council
18 Council of Lib.
19 Tax Assn.
20 Business & Ind.

Figure 3 . Community Interactive Behaviors

their audiences, the transfer of communication roles which once belonged to traditional organizations, as well as the stretching out and multiplying of communication chains. The ownership of communication facilities, the purposeful use of message design and program controls reflect the political development and philosophy of the society within which it is embedded.

INFRASTRUCTURE OF COMMUNICATION

The content of communication at any given time reflects the value pattern of the culture (65) and networks determine where information can flow and thus who can share it with whom. The orderly and balanced dissemination of communicative patterns is the responsibility of a coordinating structure. Resource agencies and their services constitute the most natural and functional coordinating structure in the community. No other agency has as broad a mandate from the people nor an influence more fundamental than media, library, and information service. The recognized elements of a coordinating structure constitute the essential foundation of the resource specializations regardless of type of administrative center:

> A service institution, such as the library must be
> closely related to its constituency, to the predom-
> inant interest of local people, to their beliefs and
> aspirations, and to their problems. The library
> must know of, and work with, the organized groups
> and established institutions which the people main-
> tain. It must study other sources of information
> and ideas and avoid unnecessary duplication of existing
> facilities while supplementing and filling gaps in the
> available intellectual resources (3).

Each community has many agencies and institutions organized to achieve social purposes or to give opportunity for the expression of varied interests. Some of these agencies are of such a fundamental importance that society gives them legal status and sanction. The library may serve as an example of an agency in American society which, since 1850 has moved from a purely voluntary and associational type of membership to full legal status and public support (116). Back in the mid-19th century when the social library was established, hopes ran high for it as "the people's university." But at best, the library has been able to serve the reading needs of only that small proportion of the population which continues to seek it out. It was not until the Library-Community

Project that librarians developed an initial competence to participate
in community life (4). However, the motivation to actually do so was
not until recently supplied and then only by younger members of the library profession in seeking for the answer to accountability.

The generalized model of a communication infrastructure (152) is
of itself not sufficient to explain the range of involvement and the functions
required of the community change agent. A second model is needed
which is based on interpersonal communication and the dynamics of community encounter. Such a model is cybernetic (105) and provides a basic
understanding of information surprise which can be applied by the floating
librarian as well as a method of comparing one communication system
with another. In order to realize the potential of the community change
agent it is necessary to move from the bounded finite infrastructures
of media, library, and information science to the role of interactive
communication systems in a dynamic environment (135).

For the floating librarian, the emphasis is on the use of information
for socioeconomic, political, and cultural purposes. Based upon knowledge as codified in the social sciences and in particular communication
science (9) there are a number of assumptions underlying the role of
the professional change agent:

> The function of criticism keeps the social system under
> control in terms of community objectives.

> Power structure response to continuous citizen criticism
> follows an ordinal distribution: (a) agreement and well-
> wishing; (b) committees and/or commissions are appointed;
> (c) economic and/or legal action occurs as a result of com-
> mittee or commission reports.

> The number of people involved in decision making varies
> directly with the range of contacts in the communication
> system.

> People are willing to use information as a social resource
> to the degree that it is perceived as an essential ingredient
> in decision making.

The encounter situations which develop among professional communicators, citizens, and community decision makers are inevitably controversial (61). The traditional librarian's credo of intellectual freedom

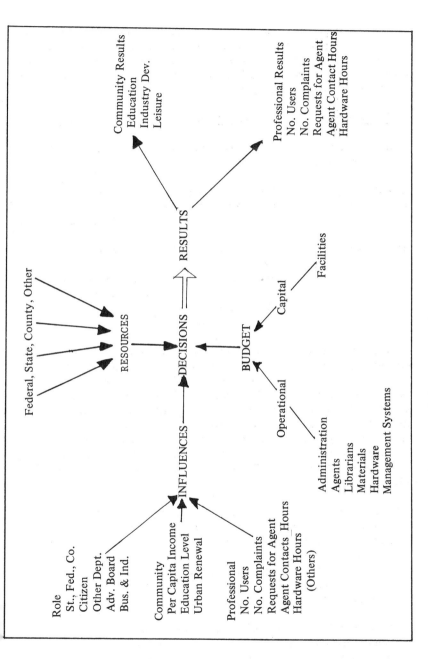

Figure 4 . Cybernetic Confrontation Components

is but a pale imitation of these dynamic learning situations and the range
in the cycle of interactions which can occur. The influences, decisions
and results are parallel to the preceptor, interpreter, and effector components of the cybernetic model of communication (see Figure 4: Cybernetic Confrontation Components).

Perceptor	Interpreter	Effector
Organized and pro- jected information	Role-structure (off- and on-line)	On-line data matrix
Mass Communication Organizations	Cognitive structure: organized information space	Land use Financial constraints
Talking chains	Affective structure: power government	Legal constraints Demographic constraints
	Skills structure: roles people play	

The confrontation is between the change agent professions and the
community power structure. In either instance, social power is the
ability to satisfy people's preferences. The real question is whether
the preferences of people will be satisfied through the negotiation of
political and economic leverages or by the opportunity for effective assembly and mediated access to appropriate information. Cunningham
(30) has discussed various methods for linking neighborhoods to city
hall which can be employed by the citizens and the various helping professions working together. Criteria for such methods include the
following:

Internal mechanisms which permit all groups within a
neighborhood the opportunity to advance their interests
and for resolving conflicts in a democratic manner

Effective decision making methods to expedite communication between neighborhoods and city hall within a
reasonable time

Citizen spokesmen should be representative of the
neighborhood by having real sanction of the people in
order to deliver on their end of the negotiations

The ideas of all individuals and groups should have a
chance of being heard at both the neighborhood and city
hall levels.

Leadership and methods of communication and negotiation
may have to be sustained over a long period of time.

Methods employed should be capable of linking one or
more neighborhoods to each other and to city hall.

The infrastructure of media, library, and information science is
not sufficient of itself to ensure that information will surprise people.
A mediating profession is needed to create conditions (or to exploit
actual conditions) which will maximize the surprise value of retrievable
data. The problem is how to arouse the curiosity level of a target audience. This means that information must be made to meet needs and
interests of an individual, a group, or a community. In effect, information can widen the involvement of people in the political and economic
power structure.

The resource communicator in the community develops programs,
whatever their names or sponsorship, which stress the citizens' participation in the improvement of their physical and social environment.
The community development approach stresses process rather than content. Changed attitudes of people are more important than the material
achievement of community projects. The scope of community development is more inclusive than education but, as a process of improving
the common life of the community, it is necessarily educational and informational.

Sociologists have long recognized that the community exerts a great
influence on the development of human personality. A democratic society
depends for its existence upon citizen participation. No better way has
been found to achieve widespread and enlightened citizen participation
than through involvement in community problems. It is here that communications programming comes alive and takes on real meaning and
purpose for the individual.

In order to nourish the development of a structure through which
the community is to be changed, people must become discontented with
existing conditions in their community (2). This involves the development
of an image of potentiality or maturity not only among leaders but as
widespread as possible among all the people. It is the responsibility

of the resource communicator as a community leader to help develop
this discontent and to inculcate the image of potentiality and maturity.

The change agent resource specialist seeks to identify and use community interest and problems for the growth and development of all people
in the community. Interests and problems become the motivations essential to the assembling of the who's which upon involvement begin to
interact with the what's. Such is the formula for translating concerns
into educational programs. Who needs to know what about this problem?
The communications change agent identifies groups (the who's) that
can use information (the what's) for a community-oriented professional
service program.

The discontent generated must be focused and channeled into organization. The floating resource specialist undertakes the task of planning
in order to meet unmet needs and to develop potentiality. But he also
develops an action program, a program designed step-by-step to develop
the potentialities of the community, as well as human and natural resources. The problems of the community are not insurmountable provided the change agent employs an appropriate organizational structure,
the proper procedure, and a fundamental action program through which
these specific problems can be solved.

Despite this analysis of community structure, the ability of the
traditional satellite group to respond to the real concerns of a wide range
of citizens has been challenged (2). There are two major reasons for
this concern. In the first place, various studies have indicated that
only slightly more than half the adult population are ever actively associated with any type of organization (33). Secondly, the traditional community structure has more often than not been manipulated by the power
structure into positions that tend to ignore fundamental issues in the community.

The power structure is usually composed of the men who have ex-
ploited the natural and industrial resources of the community and who
have mustered the people into productive work life. These individuals
dominate the economic and political life and, according to power structure
analyses (1), tend to exert a pervasive influence over the entire community in the following ways:

Keep the formal associations talking about goals and
objectives and involved with welfare and civic projects peripheral to fundamental problems.

Ensure that fundamental problems are not discussed widely in mass media or in organizational meetings.

Isolate (ignore) the professional worker from the small group in the upper reaches of power; he himself all too effectively isolates himself from average citizens.

Keep the underlying population, not normally members of formal organizations from having effective channels in order to voice their demands.

It should not be concluded that the relationship of the power structure is one of overt domination or that it consciously exerts a malign influence. It does not operate with the formality and structure of a dictatorship, but the tendency towards structure usually increases in the absense of community endeavor and towards a lack of widespread freedom of communication and education. In fact, the power structure has had to take action because most communities lack floating change agents who can involve the community in policy determination that takes into account the interests of people themselves (51).

The media, library, and information agency enjoys a unique place in the institutional structure of any community (28). As an agency of the people it is non-political, upholds no particular interest, and subscribes to complete freedom of communication and education. Consequently, resource professionals have the infrastructure base from which they can more readily work with both the power structure and the community for a better democratic way of life for all. The resource communicator uses the community coordinating structure (media, library, and information resource service) to support and strengthen the existing organizations in the community (77).

At no time should a feeling of competition be allowed to develop between the communicator and any special interest group in the community. In fact, one of his major purposes is to promote participation in special interest groups as well as develop effective leaders not only for his own service programs but also for all other organizations in the community. Each individual citizen should be considered carefully in order to understand his or her potentiality for leadership (125). Many people cannot perform effectively in one leadership position but can do so in another. The community change agent seeks out, trains, and develops leadership capacities to the fullest degree possible in every individual in the community.

DEVELOPING CONCEPT

In the minds of many media, library, and information specialists, the idea of a community change agent remains as a concept under develop- ment (94). This is to be expected where there is a considerable time lag between traditional library and professional developments in response to the discontent of emerging neighborhoods as well as demands for lay control of community libraries (120). However, Martin (90) has main- tained with some emphasis that the librarian has an essential responsi- bility as a politician.

In any event, the concept of the community change agent is not partic- ularly new in the history of librarianship, even though the term itself may be of more recent origin. Originators of the idea include Learned (74) and Wheeler (149) who, in 1924, vigorously propounded the idea of a com- munity librarian who was both an educator (Learned) and a politician (Wheeler). Actually, the public library in the United States was founded on the principles of continuing education (41) and community involvement. But it is interesting to speculate as to why these principles lay dormant for so many years. Indeed Ditzion (36) may have identified the problem when he considered that librarians were merely being shrewd in using this objective in order to win better support:

> For library interests, humanitarianism was too
> often a tactical approach to the sympathies of
> persons of influence. It was, to be sure,
> psychologically sound to appeal to human and
> social values shared by Americans in all walks
> of life.

In any event, neither the 1876 report on libraries (142) of the U.S. Office of Education which was a collection of papers about library ser- vice, nor Maddox (89) in analyzing the first ten years of the proceedings of the American Library Association seriously discuss the role of the librarian in the community. Although there was a brief attempt during the first decade of the 19th century (52) to make the university and its library the center for continuing adult education, no library until the 1920's made any serious effort to define its role in the community.

One of the first compelling statements on the library in the commun- ity was the collection of papers edited by Carnovsky and Martin (21). For the first time, one begins to sense the merger of two trends which had been developing concomitantly: the importance given to community study by Wheeler (149) as a basis for library service, and the emphasis

upon an educational role for the agency by Learned (74). The central
purpose of these papers was to counteract the habit of thinking of the
library in terms of its infrastructure as distinct from function.

It should be obvious in this presentation and in other surveys (103,
75), that the major emphasis in previous discussions of the library in
the community focused upon the library as an agency and not upon the
role of the librarian as a change agent. Walter Stone (133) was apparently
the first leader to make this important distinction. Almost immediately
thereafter, the Asheim report (7) made an attempt to elaborate this new
role for the librarian in terms of the training needs of knowledge, attitudes and skills.

However, it was not until the Library-Community Project (4) that
a concerted effort was made to train librarians for action in the community. There were a number of hypotheses which this field research project was designed to test and were subsumed under the major hypothesis
that professionals and trustees could, through involvement in the project,
learn to work more effectively in the community. A number of situations
were created to help a few "pilot" librarians to realize this objective.

The results of the Library-Community Project have not been realized
(93) principally because no theory of communication compatible with professional objectives was available to explain its contributions. This
situation has been remedied, and a theory is available (101) which is general enough to include the library and information sciences as well as
their professional competencies with the gestalt of human endeavor. A
research vehicle has been developed and its potential for canonical and
experimental research design has been described (105, 151).

In the meantime, there have been several movements for change at
the professional level. As a result of the Congress for Change in 1970,
a number of these movements began to coalesce. In her challenge paper
at the Congress, Bundy (16) outlined some of the competencies which the
librarian as change agent would need. The same theme has also been
expressed by Garrison (48). As far as can be determined, Bundy was
the first to use the term "floating librarian" for the librarian as a change
agent.

Of course, the concept of the community change agent is not new.
Agricultural Extension has developed the role of the rural community
change agent over a period of more than half a century (71). In 1950,
Sanders (121) "popularized" the competencies of the community worker

in dynamic situations. Burke (18) and Duncan (38) have developed a model
of social interaction that is more functionally oriented than the infrastructure model of Parsons (100).

There are two historically influential sources for the role of floating
librarian in the community: (1) the recent dissatisfaction with the profession among younger librarians which emerged in the 1960's and eventually found expression in the Congress for Change; (2) the sociological
inquiries of the Chicago Graduate Library School of the 1930's and 1940's
which were eventually applied to the profession in the American Heritage
and Library-Community Projects of the 1950's. Waples' study, What
Reading Does for People (144) remains as a major seminal approach to
a model of communication for the community resource change agent.

During the mid-1960's two projects were undertaken, the New Haven
and the Brooklyn experiments (43), which were catalytic in channeling
the general dissatisfaction with the librarian's role in the community.
In New Haven, a social worker was employed in one branch (26) while
in Brooklyn, professional librarians walked the streets (43) in an effort
to make library service relevant to people who had not previously used
the libraries. These developments were related to the war on poverty
(114) which is only one social imperative for the floating librarian.

Another movement which developed during the latter part of the 1960's
was based on the concept of social responsibility (11) and received formal
recognition in the New York Social Responsibilities Round Table. Although
localized in the New York area as the result of the controversy over community control of the schools in Ocean Hill-Brownsville (96), the movement towards social responsibility received widespread attention. An
attempt was made during 1968-69 to have the American Library Association
accept the Social Responsibilities Round Table as part of its formal
structure (97).

The bibliographic "pentagon" in Chicago was not able to respond that
rapidly to the wishes of its younger members and a Congress for Change
was called, June 20-22, 1969. In general, the Congress for Change was
a speculation on the role of the floating librarian as an independent information agent in the community and appeared to endorse the twin proposition
of Bundy's "manifesto" (15): decentralized and lay control of library service; as well as advocacy to achieve the library rights of people in various
settings:

One advantage to working for himself or for a client
group would be that he could more effectively place
demands on libraries and other information services
to which his clients have rightful claims. He could
indeed assume an advocacy role for his clients, being
deliberately troublesome when a library did not readily
supply services or information to which he as representing
his client is entitled.

There have been various stirring calls to social action which have
been widely discussed in the library profession such as those by Johnson
(66), Stone (133), and others. Blakeley, however, has expressed the
current challenge to the social responsibility of librarianship. According
to Blakeley (11) librarians have a choice, but have yet to commit themselves. The choice is "between continuing to try to flee individually
from our common problems and turning to face them together; between
continuing to behave like passive victims of social forces and trying to
act like positive agents in their control; between continuing to live in
accord with the 'four walls' philosophy or beginning to live in accord
with the philosophy of community renewal."

The floating librarian, both as a concept and as a function, is related
to the idea of an ombudsman or an advocate but in a sense that makes
this type of function appropriate for librarians. Even though appropriate,
it is still highly controversial to maintain that the librarian has responsibility for the surprise value of the information provided to his client.
Recognizing that limitations exist in the traditional approach of library
standards for public services, a few adult services librarians have under
development a bill of rights for adults (80, 79). While a step in the
direction of improved services, it does not get at the fundamental problem of taking responsibility for and leadership in identifying the behavioral outcomes sought by the continuing learner. If only Wheeler's objectives (149) were realized, public relations methods could serve for
initial communications programming (122).

It appears that library service to the disadvantaged has captured
the attention of today's librarians in a manner similar to the emphasis
on service to the foreign born which preoccupied the librarians in the
first quarter of this century. The priorities in service to the foreign
born have shifted to those who are also disadvantaged (139). During
the period 1964-68 over 250 articles appeared in library literature about
public library service to the disadvantaged (132). This literature is
descriptive of what librarians have been doing in developing services
(87). While it is not critical, the very nature of the services demanded

and provided have since then led a number of librarians to consider advocacy as a basic role for the profession of library and information science

A careful distinction is required between information science and communication (102) in order to understand and appreciate the change agent potential of the floating librarian. The surprise value of information is essentially entropy-reducing if and only if the information transfer endeavors of media, library and information science constitute a communications component within a situation-producing profession (34). The floating librarian defines this function for library and information science.

The librarian qua librarian has only in a latent manner the potential to be a major entropy-reducing influence in the social structure. The ideas contained in the documents may make the library the "hottest spot in town" (58) but the potential will not be realized until more floating librarians create situations that will make people dissatisfied with present services. Traditional library service has, of course, organized that part of information space (i.e. the published record) which is most amenable to logical organization but which is least sought after for information surprise by most people. There is a whole area of information space developed and determined by the present moment, the immediate past, and the impending future (futurology) which not only remains unorganized but is avidly sought after by the majority of people. In these areas information surprise means power.

Power is an inescapable factor in the affairs of men. Whereas power in the physical sciences is the energy to do work, power in the social realm is the ability to satisfy wants. Conceptually, the floating librarian has unlimited power and is constrained directly only by his ability to organize the totality of information space and to create conditions wherein information surprise can occur for the greatest number of people (55, 67).

There appears to be an irrevocable clash between this power to satisfy wants through information and the economic power which governments can exercise in order to ameliorate the condition of all people. Indeed at this level of development the library profession is but dimly aware of the problem. Its "precious" so-called contemporary intellectual freedom stance is but an effete and superficial shadow of the confrontation challenges which the floating librarian must face in his daily activities.

The floating librarian as a community librarian has captured some of the enthusiasm and dynamic involvement which has been demonstrated so effectively and for so many years by the Agricultural Extension Agents (52). In applying these and other methods to the urban situation, the floating librarian is helping the library realize some of the hope for it (now more than a century old!) as a focal point for the people's university and as a learning laboratory for the entire community. All life influences can be educational and to make them increasingly effective the floating librarian has found that many educational forces in the community must be marshalled simultaneously (17, 86).

The floating librarian values the role of the activist as an essential and necessary ingredient in the healthy life of any community. While he may upon occasion be an irritant to the majority of moderate citizens, without the activist the community would not be as desirable a place to live (2). The activist becomes involved in whatever role can be counted upon to irritate the public's fancy. His major method is iconoclasm and his patron saint is Thersites of Grecian lore. Whatever proposal is make even in his own group, the activist is vociferous in denouncing it and champions a diametrically opposing position which is, of course, a minority position.

As a consequence, a dialectical situation is created which forces the real issues and assumptions to be examined and defended. From this conflict situation new ideas or alternatives are synthesized that are frequently far superior to either of the original ones.

Often the new proposal, when it is made and as it begins to shape up, appears to be a concession to radicalism. But as one begins to examine it more closely one finds that the substance of the proposal remains in the camp of the moderates while the dramatic externals are designed to palliate the wishes of the activist's more radical constituents. Thus the activist and the moderate complement one another, but it takes the moderate to follow through and implement the dramatic and intuitive insights of the activist (61).

The floating librarian keeps his community under continuous review in order to identify the variety of teachable moments which make the timing of informational and educational efforts productive. By involving an increasingly wider range of adults in community study, the librarian is determining subject areas in which the library and other community agencies can prepare "units" or program development for "curricular" study (17). The immediate program planning of agencies, organizations, and groups shifts in accordance with the progressive, cooperative identification of community problems and interests. The librarian becomes an active educator applying professional insight to community problems out where it is needed most, beyond the library walls (110).

The library is no longer just an agency. The floating librarian uses it as a __method__ for aiding people to learn continuously. A community related library can provide an improved community-wide background. People learn better and faster when the knowledge sought is closely related to everyday activities in the community (60). This is evident in the fact that the programming of television networks is beginning to have almost as potent an influence on the citizen as his actual community background (8).

Recognizing their adult liberal education responsibility to the community, librarians also begin the slow process of making it difficult for the majority of people to avoid thinking about the issues in the community and in the world at large:

> No matter how well one is acquainted with the community in which he lives, a fresh and searching look, a reshuffling of the available facts, will bring new insights. The process of looking at the community may be regarded as taking stock, an attempt to map the present position before deciding on new destinations. Comprehensive and specific knowledge of the characteristics of the people making up the community, the circumstances under which they live, and the extent and kinds of change that are taking place will help in estimating their capabilities and their interests; it will provide clues as to both the nature and underlying causes of their problems, and those of the community at large (113).

MODELS AND METHODS

The unique characteristic of the floating librarian is in the role of a change agent. A new dimension is added to the profession when the resource specialist takes responsibility for helping people determine a desirable range of changed behaviors for themselves. The traditional retrieval and program skills which respond to demand are inadequate in the new context (5). Even the concept of intellectual freedom remains an effete notion to people who are disadvantaged and discontent (119). Such people want advocacy (15) before they can ever be expected to seek out the opportunity to read widely and for self-maturation.

In contrast to the rather passive role of most librarians, the change agent has responded more positively to the task of fulfilling human

aspiration and accomplishing social purpose. In order to offset the pre-
ponderence of bureaucratic elements which are inherent in any infrastructure (136), the floating librarian movement is at the moment attempting to organize its advocacy functions into the more formal role of
ombudsman. Citizens who are insecure and lack social support need a
professional service to lend them its strength and resources (19). Neighborhood information and other types of centers have been developed,
even though the problems of institutionalization and bureaucracy are
beginning to appear.

To offset the limitations of structure and maximize his role as advocate, the floating librarian may have to be attached to some ombudsman's
agency whose sole purpose is to investigate citizen complaints (150).
The need for an opportunity to redress individual grievances may be
widely recognized (20), but it will not be easy for many. Perhaps only
a few·select librarians will transfer from a library to an ombudsman's
agency where of necessity materials and bibliographies may have to be
forgone (147). The management of a bibliographic apparatus of any sort
would probably cripple the effectiveness of a change agent.

Professional reactions to the new social imperatives have ranged
from injured consternation at the "evident" ingratitude among younger
librarians, to the mea culpas over the lack of social relevance in librarianship (10). A sense of introspection has developed in the profession
because the usual training of librarians has not prepared them for the
dynamics of planned change (84, 109). Indeed the profession at large
has never seriously considered the role of the change agent, let alone
developed models of communication that would lay a foundation for appropriate implementation.

At one point in the history of community development education, it
used to be necessary to raise the discontent level of people in the neighborhoods before much involvement and action would result. But today
most community situations have changed. People are already discontent
and frequently involved in indigenous action programs. It is rather the
resource specialists themselves who will have to change (44) whether
as a salesman, community coordinator, or change agent (98).

The social problem cannot be avoided. Individual libraries and
especially librarians are struggling to define a role for themselves under
rapidly changing conditions (123). Out of the activist ferment, the intellectual creativity, and group confrontation sessions have emerged a new
emphasis in the professional specializations of the community worker
and the floating librarian. In fact, it appears that there are four principal
models of the communications librarian in the community.

The first model is that of the "outreach project." Outreach or extension services reverse the tendency of many agency programs which expect patrons to come to the main or branch building for service. Of course, the concept of library extension is not a new method in the profession. But librarians have recently experimented with a greater variety of techniques, such as storefront libraries, drugstore collections, reading stations, book vans. In most instances, these outreach projects have distributed types of ephemeral and audiovisual materials that until a few years ago were not included in library collections. In addition, the staffing of such projects has included indigenous people who are more attuned to the social mores of the neighborhoods.

The second model of the community librarian includes the type of community involvement which was developed principally by the American Heritage Project and the Library-Community Project. The institutional stance developed in this model is grounded in the historical objectives and standards of the profession. Community development education is based on the premise that the community is the matrix of a liberal education for all citizens. In other words, the involvement of citizens is a major educational method whose purpose is to create a climate of community life wherein the continuous learning of all people can occur.

The third model is that of the community librarian whose role is not curtailed by regular hours within the library. The daily schedule of this community worker is so freed that he can work to meet the emerging needs and interests of people in the community when and where these occur. The role of this type of resource specialist is a catalytic change agent. It may include the role of advocacy but not the function of ombudsman. Exerting information leadership, he labors with those who work for changes that will better all those citizens who are psychologically disadvantaged. This means all community people, black and white, poor and rich; for as Brock Chisholm says, "There are no problems which do not exist, except in the minds of people."

The final model is truly one of a change agent whose purpose is to meet the informational needs of his client groups. This role includes the concept of advocacy as well as the concept of the ombudsman. As an ombudsman, the change agent could be employed by any office that is established to coordinate the advocacy functions needed by a community. In any event, this professional person is adept at ferreting out information where it lies hidden in any agency, institution, or the most "public" of library infrastructures. Ralph Nader, for example, has effectively utilized this model for his inquiries into consumer affairs and has shown that it is a workable model.

Whichever model of his role, or combination of them, a change agent chooses to use in guiding his activity in the community, the profession at least in "theory" has long held certain social objectives. The community is considered to be a marketplace of ideas as well as a learning center where the citizen may explore divergent avenues of social change. The role of the professional person is to stimulate the articulation possible in relevant and orderly decision-making processes. Librarians have held to a concept of the community as the matrix of a liberal education for all who participate in its affairs.

While there may be several models of the librarian in the community, there appear to be two essential functions of the floating librarian: the advocate and the ombudsman. The function of ombudsman is to coordinate the various advocacy services available to the citizen and to lodge formal complaints. The library has prided itself upon its nonsectarian and nonpolitical role in the community. As such, the library is in an enviable position as the coordinator of information sources and the services of the organized community.

As distinct from objectives or procedures, methods are the general ways or motivational devices by which a profession creates relationships between the knowledge and information it has to diffuse and the concerns and interests of people. The major communicative methods of the floating librarian can be organized around Dickoff's (34) five functional areas in any profession: agency, patron, objective, method, protocol. Each of these general methods can encompass a wide range of interface communicative activity.

Communicative method one includes the continuous study of needs and concerns of individuals, groups and communities by community study (total community); audience research (reached users of library); market analysis (unreached publics). The requirements of market and audience research are partially met as the functions of a coordinating structure begin to operate. The community needs, resources, and services are made known to the community as a whole. Out-of-community resources are obtained as soon as the need for them is anticipated. Services are developed that will motivate people to participate in information surprise experiences. Media are so orchestrated into a comprehensive communications program which will saturate the community, make it difficult for people to avoid thinking about the issues of concern, and get the "talking chains" going in the community.

Communicative method two includes the identification and securing of community and out-of-community resources. Resources include all

human, printed, and audio-visual materials recorded and published in
the public domain; resource persons, agencies, organizations; present
moment developments on the mass media. Most metropolitan areas are
rich in information resources, both general and specialized. Major resource centers have begun to work together through a network in order
to avoid unnecessary duplication of collections and to facilitate access
both to their own resources and to other libraries in the national network.

In communicative method three, the resource change agent helps to
improve the programs of the agencies and organizations, by co-sponsoring
programs in areas of concern where programs are not now under development; surveying resource production to identify lacunae in knowledge;
and promoting research in areas of concern not researched or developed
with a published record (141). These basic problems are still unattended
and with each passing year become more imperative (40). There is a
need in most communities and in the metropolitan area, especially for
indexes to information spaces that exist in ephemeral and mission-oriented sources and materials.

In communicative method four, the floating librarian makes it difficult for all people to avoid thinking about personal, group and community issues. A multitude of stimuli are presented on the mass media, so
that the social endeavor becomes a community programmed for communication and learning. Professional librarians are stationed at points
where they can immediately interface with patrons whether on the premise
or out of the community. These librarians are skilled in interviewing,
guidance counseling, group and community work. They are prepared
in educational psychology and communications for dyad, group, and community contexts:

> In the Dyad, professional librarians are needed who can work
> with all age groups and interests in order to: listen, encourage,
> and stimulate person(s) to think about their problem; label
> and define the problem or experience; develop synonyms for
> flexibility; negotiate files for retrieval.

> In the Group, these librarians develop sequential exper-
> iences on a predetermined topic of concern in order to:
> counsel for group processes; train for leadership and
> role productivity; respect other viewpoints and develop
> ability to handle other value systems "objectively";
> transcend negative group roles.

In the Community, the floating librarian serves as a communications leader in order to create a saturation awareness and stimulate information surprises; motivate participation by "needling" the value system(s) of the community; motivate learning by involvement; follow-up by
preparing specific materials to meet particular purposes.

In communicative method <u>five</u> the effectiveness of library services
is evaluated. Categories of evaluation which serve as the performance
categories include: new audiences (groups) reached; increased county
legislation for social issues; increased (or reallocated) county budget
for social issues; increased per capita library income; increased effectiveness of satellite groups; speed of out-of-community access; increase in number and range of out-of-community resources; decrease
and lack of censorship problems; overcoming type of library service.

The overriding concern in these five methods is the dichotomy between the creation of new knowledge and the use of it by a communicative
change agent. The purpose of knowledge generation is to achieve order
through the predictive power of an orderly research procedure. The
purpose of communication, on the other hand, is to make the predictive
power of knowledge kinetic in the affairs of men. The findings of the
sciences are related to the purposes of society, groups, and individuals
by the various professions. Such normative and prescriptive functions
of a communicative profession have been expressed in the above set of
standards for a coordinating profession.

The goals of a coordinating structure can be developed out of the
actual needs of the community. These goals, to be understood, must
provide a strong motivating force for people joining together to meet
common needs and the general methods and procedures must be acceptable
to the people. The methods and the general procedures to be acceptable
must be worked out from the goals of the particular community. These
goals must have wide acceptability, and be understood by all the people
in order to avoid the tendency among many communities for the goals to
be placed in the background. In such instances, the particular action
projects become ends in themselves. This is an educational job which
must be carried on continuously in every organized community.

FIVE

MONITORING CONCERNS AND INTERESTS

The community is, in general, a large and amorphous entity with which it is difficult if not impossible to work. Systematic plans have to be developed for the articulation and analysis of concerns and interests which in turn can be employed as guidelines for program and message design. The underlying causes for consumer action have to be investigated by methods more sophisticated than those which assume that consumers understand and can identify the causes of their own actions. In any event the principal holds: that which makes a community change are the articulated concerns and interests.

Had librarians more generally risen to the opportunity offered to them by the Library-Community Project of the American Library Association, the sudden transition to the present decade of accountability and lay control might have been more developmental and educational for a wider range of citizen volunteers. Instead of being forced into violent administrative confrontation with activists, the community-library relations should have become a behavioral environment programmed for discovery learning. Certainly the methods and programs of agency-community development, when implemented by resource communicators, create the conditions wherein all citizens can continue their own self-development and education.

Some predictions of things to come are needed and of the trends which get us from here to there. It is difficult to see how such trends can be described without the help of some wise "experts." It would be better not to have to use them, because their reliability is not particularly high. This approach depends upon the projections of broadly informed and intelligent persons who can be asked to give estimates of how much leisure time people will have in the future, how many tasks will be performed by computer systems, how daily lives will be affected by changes in the arts of communication. Resource informants who have been found useful in this endeavor included directors of adult education, special field advisory committees, temporary committees, guidance officials, joint lay and faculty committees, and boards of education. In fact, many individuals and groups can help in the major task of identifying the needs and interests of the community and should be encouraged to do so.

No matter how well one is acquainted with the community in which he lives, a fresh and searching look, a reshuffling of the available facts, will bring new insights. The process of looking at the community may be regarded as taking stock, an attempt to map the present position before deciding on new destinations. Comprehensive and specific knowledge of the characteristics of the people making up the community, the circumstances under which they live, and the extent and kinds of change that are taking place will help in estimating their capabilities and their interests; it will provide clues as to both the nature and the underlying causes of their problems, and those of the community at large (113).

Some method is needed for determining goals. Such goals, particularly in today's world of rapid societal change, must be forward-looking. Results based upon people's concrete experience do not necessarily indicate this kind of orientation to the future. The functions of a communications "elite" identify and give expression to community concerns and interests that are as yet inchoate and only dimly perceived. One must, therefore, somehow take account of the changes in communications and media, in computerization of work, and in probable increases in leisure time.

The communicator will have to master the institutional techniques necessary to bring together the segments of the intellectual, industrial and technological community required to identify and meet goals in a planned fashion. Some system is required in order to realize the substantial investments which have been made in communications technology and in order to channel these efforts towards programs of social significance. In order to offset the fragmented approaches of the past towards the communicative enterprise, the following steps should be taken on a community-wide basis:

Identify clear goals by involving as many segments of the community as possible.

Institutionalize the mechanisms for achieving such goals around the functions of a coordinating structure.

Engage all segments of the community whose talents and resources can be employed to realize these goals.

Identify and assemble the markets or publics who can be motivated to become involved with appropriate services and communication programs.

The development of a systems approach to communication and learning must begin with a study to determine goals. This is necessary because it is from a statement of the goals of a system that all the logic of this approach flows. One could, of course, have these goals determined by a panel of "experts," and this would not be an entirely unreasonable approach. But, insofar as a program of communication services is to be instituted by a community, it seems wise to attempt to determine what the needs are of this segment of society. Kempfer (69) has identified one plan for the specification of consumer concerns and interests:

Cultivation of "coordinator" or liaison people in industry, business, and community organizations who watch for opportunities for education to perform a service

Receiving requests from business, industrial, labor and community groups for information and communication services

Study of learning deficiencies among adult consumers as well as their behavioral patterns in negotiating index space

Maintenance of extensive personal acquaintance with community leaders and groups

Examination of census and similar data from available surveys and histories of this and other communities

Making systematic surveys of industrial, business, and civic life of the community

Examination of catalogs, schedules, publicity materials, reports and programs of other informational and communicative agencies in the community

Being sensitive to civic, personal, and social problems of people which could be alleviated by education, information, and communication

Such efforts cannot be accomplished simply by means of superficial "survey" techniques. A sophisticated line of questioning based on some research design should be followed, in order to come as close as possible to "true" needs. In order to get closer to true needs, it is necessary to ask questions based upon the premise that learning means a change in capability. Questions need to be developed that are designed to reveal concrete instances of desire or felt need (on the part of those questioned) for changing their capabilities. Such categories might be very different from the names of services offered by a particular agency. In this process of determing the goals of communication and learning it is self defeating to impose preexisting, and possibly quite obsolete, categories upon the results.

The determination of broad general goals is an essential and preliminary step to be taken. The goals then need to be categorized further in terms of the human functioning such as the classes of human performance. One would need to develop categories of what kinds of human capabilities are involved and for some range of human beings included in the broad goal for example of increased occupational competence. These might include such behavioral outcomes as communication capabilities, human relations capabilities, numerical, and quantitative capabilities. Such performance classes might bear some relation to the categories of "academic" subject matters, such as language and mathematics. But just because these traditional categories have grown up around the education of youth, and seem to represent a kind of stable reality, is no reason to suppose that exactly the same categories would emerge in consideration of continuing learning requirements.

At any rate, broad goals need to be broken down into more specific categories of objectives. If learning is the purpose of the system, it cannot be conceived as a process without relating it to observable performances. Indeed, if a system is to be developed, it must be designed with the aim of producing specific outcomes, and that is really just another name for objectives. The goals for communication services should be determined by a rational interaction of various sources of information. From the past, it is possible to take the most highly concrete and empirically based information to be found, derived from answers to questions about actual needs. From projections into the future, the most highly informed wisdom available could be employed. But it should be a rational melding of these two kinds of information which could be expected to give the best formulation of the broad goals for a system of continuing learning and communication.

Citizens scatter here and there; the communicator has trouble reaching them, especially when their concerns are marked by the strident demands of the advocate. Each adult moves forward not only chronologically, but from role to role as he leaves childhood and becomes a worker, an adult member of a family and a voting citizen. The communicator of today must know how adult needs for knowledge are revealed.

He will not find all of the adults gathered at given times into neat groups.
He cannot talk with each individual in the library — too many never use
the library. Indeed only a percentage of them ever attend the meetings
of clubs and organizations. The communicator must look at his community in order to identify the variety of teachable moments which make the
timing of informational and educational efforts productive.

> When the body is ripe, and society requires, and the self
> is ready to achieve certain tasks, the teachable moment
> has come. Efforts at teaching which would have been largely
> wasted if they had come earlier, give gratifying results when
> they come at the teachable moment, when the task should
> be learned (57).

To arrive at anything like a representative list of teachable moments in any community may be a physical impossibility. Surely it will
be a continuing and continuous process for the resource communicator.
A start must be made somewhere. The communicator, staff, trustees
and citizens can begin to study the community, identify and describe
probable areas of community concern. Every citizen is aware of certain inadequacies in his communal life. The community study attempts
to discover these needs. Usually awareness of a problem stimulates
some action on the part of some group or individual in the community.

The community study, the interviews, and the sampling survey are
examples of means by which problems can be delineated and objectively
described. Once the areas of community concern are evident, the basic
formula for identifying the educational needs can be asked: who needs
to know what about this? If anyone needs to know anything, the librarian
has an educational responsibility to meet. Once the most pressing
needs have been selected, the resource communicator, staff, trustees,
and citizens can begin to explore the implications of the need and the
existence, or perhaps lack of resources to meet that need. When the
educational need is revealed, the teachable moment has come and individuals or groups can be motivated to learn; programs can be developed
and local resources utilized.

Community study helps to strengthen the resource center as a
learning laboratory for the community and in developing a wide variety
of activities and experiences for citizens which are as important as the
utilization of subject materials. Becoming involved in community study
increases the desire of librarians to learn more about educational methods
and techniques which can be applied in meeting a variety of interests.

In the process the resource center remains no longer just an agency but becomes a method for aiding people to learn continuously and emerges as a group of services centered around a collection of materials.

The immediacy of the challenge makes some thinking imperative by the resource agencies' trustees and staff. Before they can ask citizens to help them, communicators have to know for what reasons and between what guidelines the study is to be done. Librarians and trustees, especially those in smaller libraries, find it a revelation to have to think in terms of delegating authority, before they demand it, to citizen groups who are invited to participate. The purpose of having a citizens' committee is defeated if every move of the committee must, in effect, be "authorized" by the agency's staff or board of trustees.

The total community is also in need of orientation. Eventually and by degrees it should be involved in the total educational process which is community development. The librarian attempts to meet this need by newspaper publicity, talks before groups, and displays and programs in or out of the resource center. The citizens' committee members, being themselves community leaders, can do much word-of-mouth publicity. Besides the publicity, many citizens must be directly involved in doing various phases of the study.

This involvement of people in activities associated with the resource center is educational by intent. It is not done simply to overcome the limitations of tax support. Such citizen involvement helps to keep the center closer to all the people. Citizens accept change more readily when they themselves have determined the need for it. The community development approach to information utilization and educational programming, instead of being a mere concession to democracy, is based on sound communication principles and includes the cybernetic and systems models of communication.

Citizens are articulate concerning their awareness of community needs and problems. In addition, they have time to play an increasingly important role in determining study methods best suited to the community. Members of the community study committee exert leadership in the interpretation of the study findings and in the development of the agency's service programs. Their recommendations are such that the door is opened to other agencies and organizations but especially to the people to participate.

The librarian and the staff seek to relate the facts learned about the community to the kind of communication service already available. They

measure the job now being done against the needs discovered and plan
service to citizens and the community around this combination of information. Not only are the service programs changed but the materials
collection becomes user-oriented and access is provided to extensive
local resources. Purchases are made in order to make it more adaptable to local conditions in degree of literacy, mentality and culture of
the people. In addition, the services of the agency are strengthened
by a knowledge and use of many additional resources throughout the
community.

ENVIRONMENTAL SURVEILLANCE

The functional operations of any community point out factors which
influence communications and educational program design. The people
of a community are usually interested in the extent and efficiency of essential community services. Local government is of interest to everyone. It speaks for and affects the entire community. It relates to the
health, education, and welfare of all citizens. During recent years its
activities in these areas have markedly increased. The floating librarian
should continuously study local government in order that his communicatior
and his programs may deal with timely activities. This will bring increased knowledge of government to the people, and prepare them to
participate more fully in the solutions to community problems.

The economic structure determines the level of community living,
the breadth and depth of community activities. It provides the means
by which people meet their basic needs for food, clothing, and shelter
and determines the extent to which they can go beyond that point. The
economic structure of a community often produces more problems than
any other segment of community life. Recent research has shown that
the dominant forces in the power structure of a community are clearly
centered within its economic structure. The floating librarian's job is
to identify and understand the problems that exist within the economic
structure of his community, and to deal with these problems through
the machinery of communication and education. An atmosphere should
be created in which such problems can be faced realistically and worked
out democratically by community groups.

Population data helps to predict future trends. The number and kinds
of people in a community influence social living. Programs of various
social agencies in the community are affected by changes in population,
size, and characteristics. The age and sex of the population may
greatly affect the community's organized life. The number and kind of

Table 2 . Behavior Environment Index

MATRIX	STATISTIC	SOURCE
Interpersonal laws of behavior roles of group behavior; what to say in context.	Population characteristics and types; sociocultural segments and pockets.	Census reports; histories; sociocultural groups.
Environmental laws of behavior; earning a living; using and adjusting to physical resources; changing and producing things.	Inventories of raw materials add manufactured goods; distribution of business services.	Census by manufacture and employment; vocational and professional training.
Institutional laws of behavior in organized events as a member or participant; establishing a business or other enterprise.	Character of local government and business climate; candidates for public office and civic groups.	Surveys of agency and membership organizations; zoning, housing, welfare, education, libraries.
Information space and message design laws of behavior; ability to use indexes and messages for problem-solving, creative and critical thinking.	Educational level and distribution; cultural activity and group participation; communication resources for referral.	Mass media; recreation; educational opportunity; museums, art galleries, concert halls.

people in a community influence social living. In general, the greater
the degree of concentration of people in a given area, the greater the
degree of specialization. A prevailing high degree of specialization will
influence program design, while comparative isolation makes participation
and involvement in the program more difficult to achieve.

Population education level influences community welfare, particularly
in its civic, social, and vocational aspects. Participation in community
affairs is usually correlated with level of native ability; and the higher
the level of education, the greater the extent of participation. The nature
and structure of community organizations as well as the patterns of affiliation are also strongly influenced by levels of education. Uneducated,
unskilled persons live differently (in many respects) from the more
highly educated industrial technicians and professional persons. Widespread discrepancies of this type tend to produce major areas of community tensions.

Some point of reference may prove helpful to librarians who have
not previously considered library and community study as a method for
developing more effective community service programs. The following
questions point up initial considerations in getting the community study
underway: How will the facts be gathered and organized to reveal community trends? Who will identify resources and organize information
about them for use? Who will interpret the facts in order to identify the
educational needs? Who will be invited to develop program goals, methods,
and techniques to be used in satisfying the educational needs? Who will
establish the goals, methods and techniques of evaluation?

Setting goals and establishing guidelines have been found to be essential steps in keeping the study within manageable proportions and
moving productively. The over-all guidelines will raise questions, the
answers to which will help the library promote continuing adult self-
education. These questions are not of a specific, factual nature. Answers to them rest in factual information, but for the most part, they
go beyond the more obvious aspects of a locality. The answers will be
found as a result of the processes of gathering, organizing, evaluating,
and interpreting the data.

The process of finding answers to questions such as these is educative
both to individuals and the community as people become involved in self-
study and in interpreting findings. The process of working together to
identify problems, needs, and resources common to the community will
help create the necessary machinery and organization. This is an

important step towards realizing the objectives of a community study: recognizing potentialities latent in community resources, and discovering ways to realize these potentialities. In the process the library establishes itself as a leader in the community.

An outline for community study can help librarians and adult educators in carrying out their responsibilities for educational and communications program planning. A carefully planned outline suggests the kinds of information and data about the community which will be needed by the librarian and his staff. Of course, neither the content of any outline nor the list of suggested sources of information can be considered complete or adequate for all situations. In fact, portions of the general outline may not be applicable, or be of negligible importance. Variations between communities require that the general outline include a variety of information so that applications can be made of appropriate parts.

Census reports: evidence of change, e.g., comparison of 1950-60-70 data; high and lows; variations from state and national norms

Maps, guides, handbooks, directories: physical and economic characteristics; relationships to surrounding area

Histories: patterns of cultural change, e.g., coming of new population stock, opening of transportation to other communities; development of tradition, e.g., leaders always from one social group, or wide representation in leadership; development of institutions and activities

Groups with common characteristics such as homogeneous neighborhoods, race or national groups, age groups, special interest groups, vocational groups: is this group unusual in size or nature? has it developed recently? do social agencies exist to serve it? is it represented in government and organizational membership? does it have and use educational and cultural opportunities? what is the community attitude towards it?

Community studies done by other agencies, businesses, organizations: reason for status quo, change and community characteristics; selection of pressing problems; recommendations for action; projection into the future

Various agencies — governmental and educational, voluntary
and commercial: purposes, programs and activities; requirements for and analysis of participants (age, sex, education,
income group); materials used in program planning and their
sources (nature and quality of materials); resources needed
or desirable

Business and Industry: type of manufacturing process, or
business and employee skills needed; extent and quality of
on-the-job training (points where printed or other materials
can shorten or enrich the program); resources available,
needed or desirable

Membership organizations and church groups: purpose, programs, and activities; requirements for membership and
analysis of membership; or desirable methods used in program
development; problems in meeting goals; methods of evaluation.

Mass Media — newspapers, radio, TV: educational
features, analysis of content, editorials, letters to the
editor; community response; plans for expanding educational activities; resources needed or desirable

Interviews, comments by community representatives and
general public: knowledge or lack of knowledge of documented fact; expressed attitudes on community problems
and interests; opinions on community needs

The major elements of the project include a study of the library, a
study of the community, and the development of service programs based
on the findings of the study. Studies are made of the library and the community to determine what kind of job is being done in relation to the educational goals of the library. The study involves the library staff, the
trustees, and a citizens' committee in addition to many volunteers.
Until the appearance of the community study method, librarians have
not involved volunteers in the library's informational and educational
enterprise, nor like Saul Alinsky have they encouraged them to bridge
the gap between the moderate radical of former years and the revolutionary radical of the present generation.

To determine what educational services the community lacks, as
well as what resources are available, the community resources (educational, informational, recreational) will have to be located by the

library and the citizens' committee. Many formal adult education courses, and informal educational opportunities may already be available. A variety of materials, resources, and methods are used by organizations in programming. Many organizational needs may emerge in the process as the library becomes the community's coordinating structure, such as the better utilization of all community resources for program planning. A resource file may be needed, which will provide an index to the human, printed, and audio-visual resources available in the county.

The kinds of resources sought are: human consultants (about programs, unmet needs, further resources, advisory help on library adult education problems): speakers, panel members, role-players, script and publicity writers, etc.; printed materials: books, pamphlets, manuals, newspapers, reading lists, discussion guides, etc.; audiovisual materials: films, slides, filmstrips, spoken and musical recordings. Related to resources is the important objective of locating groups which are organized around special interests or common purposes, or particular goals that fall within the educational function of the library. The important factors to find out about any agency or organization as a resource are: purpose of the group; the main activities it sponsors; the outstanding members, leaders and others who have special skills and knowledges.

Sources of resources — libraries, book stores, newsstands, film and record distributors; nature of material — books, films; quality of material; terms of use — loan, rental, purchase; extent of use and analysis of users

Sources of information — mass media, agencies (libraries), organizations, churches, newspapers, radio, TV, bulletins, newsletters

News source: announcements of coming events, personnel; emphasis on types of news, problems, achievements; bulletins, newsletter

Educational features: community response; plans for expanding educational activities; resources needed or desirable

Library informational service: reference service; community reference service; extent of use and analysis of users

Sources of educational and cultural experiences — concerts,
art exhibits, literary programs, various programs (formal
and informal for adults, agency sponsored programs, self-
education through information, library, and media centers:
type and number; cost and availability; opportunities for
participation; extent of use and analysis of users

Communities are characterized by the things in which people are
interested, the situations, qualities, or conditions they value. Such
community values may be hard to identify. But they are important to
the floating librarian who is trying to work professionally with the community in any type of informational, educational, or action program.
Communications and educational programs are doomed when they simply
do not fit into the dominant values in the community.

DATA ORGANIZATION

The values of the people living in the community are made evident
by organizing the study data to show trends. These trends indicate interests or concerns. Interests grow out of the work and recreational
life of the people and are quite often evident in mass media programming.
Some of the underlying factors include:

Factors causing change in the community — institutions or
activities which can help the community adapt to change,
or can help to forestall undesirable change

Factors limiting the community in its development, and
those which contribute to the development of the community

Factors producing tension in the community — institutions
or activities which can help to resolve the tension or to
develop desirable action from it

Community concerns or problems, on the other hand, grow out of
factors causing change especially in the distribution of economic and
political power. For example, the power structure may be a limiting
factor or demonstrate inability to diversify the means of livelihood in
the community. Tensions may also develop as the population increases
or changes in its composition. It may become increasingly difficult to
relate the potential or actual contribution of one population segment to
others. Such a condition favors the emergence of vociferous special
interest groups and the concomitant organizations formed to advocate
special interests.

Community interests are usually evident, although they may
not have been recognized by some agencies. Clues to interests may be found in the study of attendance at commercial
shows (even at a distance from the community), response to
TV and radio programs, reading of special magazines, membership in special interest organizations, responses to certain
questions.

When strong interests are recognized as responsibilities,
action is usually taken. However, there may be a lack of
coordination. Some interests may be overlooked or inadequately served such as those interests held by fewer people,
or seldom expressed because of lack of encouragement may
have been overlooked or inadequately served. New interests
constantly emerge as the community, the nation and the
world change.

A trend in the community is evident when no institution or activity
exists to recognize inadequacies, change, and tension, and to guide
the community in its reaction to them. Existing institutions or activities may be inadequate to meet such a situation. They may be overlapping in their efforts, or are not coordinating their efforts — a problem which viable community library service can overcome. There
may also be groups with common characteristics who do not participate
in community life, or who do not benefit from community activities by
their own choice, by community action, or because of community attitudes. Problems exist largely in the minds of people, but they may
become manifest when:

No institution or activity exists to recognize inadequacies,
change, and tension, and to guide the community in its reaction to them. Do they recognize a responsibility?

Existing institutions or activities are inadequate to meet
the situation, or are overlapping in their efforts, or are
not coordinating their efforts.

Groups with common characteristics do not participate in
community life, or do not benefit from community activities
by their own choice, by community action, or because of
community attitudes.

Table 3. Community Data Organization

I Problem area (trend) or concern	II Evidence	III Community resources available
A lack of appreciation for continuing education and of facilities for it.	Data: 45% of people have an 8th grade education or less. Predominance of younger people who do not use the public library as much as the older age groups. Lower education group does not use the public library. Financial support of information, library and media centers is low. Absence of a clearing-house of information about educational resources and programs	Greater University Extension TV classes for illiterates TV classes on high school level City and county school boards Information, Library and Media Centers
A lack of a sense of over-all community responsibility by the majority of the population.	Data: Presidential voting is low. Predominance of younger people who do not belong to organizations Crime rate is high Automobile accident rate is increasing	Various organizations Churches Governmental agencies Red Cross
High crime and accident rate	Data: Crime rate High percentage of young males Interviews - Lack of cooperation between city and county Fact - No car inspection	Driver training program Juvenile court Alcoholics Anonymous

An evaluation of the likelihood that a trend actually exists may be indicated by two criteria. The first is the authority of the source, e.g., census figures against opinion; record of a professional agency as against a record of a membership organization. The second is the frequency with which it appears in the data, e.g., need for better group relations as shown in geographic segregation, social discrimination, variations in income levels between groups as well as need for coordination of community efforts as shown by overlapping agency services, competitive organizational efforts, and lack of adequate communication among groups.

The involvement of citizens in activities in association with community development is educational by intent. It is not done simply to over-

come the limitations of tax support. Such citizen involvement helps to
keep the social agencies closer to all the people. Citizens accept change
more readily when they themselves have determined the need for it.
The community development approach to information utilization and educational programming, instead of being a mere concession to democracy,
is based on sound communication principles and includes the cybernetic
and systems models of communication.

DATA EVALUATION

Every individual reflects his community, especially the community
in which he grew up. What sort of individuals, what sort of people in
the future, will flow from the library community? Will they have an adequate image of their own potentiality? Will their leadership capacities
be fully developed? Will they participate actively in community life
wherever they go? Each library and especially each public service
librarian is responsible in part for each individual in the community as
well as those who flow out from the community.

Communities are characterized by the things in which people are
interested: the situations, qualities, or conditions they value. Such
community values may be hard to identify. But they are important to
the communicator who is trying to work professionally with the community in any type of informational, educational, or action program. Communications and educational programs are doomed when they are not
related to the dominant value patterns in the community. Basic values
in the community must be identified and programs must subsequently be
designed in terms of these values which may be inferred from the answers to questions such as the following:

The Population

Are more people moving out of the community than are moving into
it? Are young people leaving the city? Is there a disproportionate number of men or women in the population? Are there crowded or slum areas
within the city limits? Are the residential, commercial, and industrial
areas clearly zoned? Are there racial or national groups that do not
participate in community life?

In planning for future service, which age groups are likely to need
increased volume of service? Which age groups promise to increase

sharply in size? What racial and national groups make up this population? Have proportions changed or shifted in the past thirty years among national and racial groups?

What is the range and median level of income of families and unrelated individuals, as listed in the census figures? What income groups form the largest proportion of the population? Do building permits indicate accelerated building of homes, and what is the average size and cost? Is the community changing? How fast, in what respects and sections? Has there been a sizeable population influx in recent years? Where did people come from? How well are they integrated into the community? How are minority groups being assisted in integration?

Economic Life

How much unemployment is there in the community? What kinds of businesses and industries operate in the community? What kinds of jobs do people have? What is the range of consumer income? To what extent are economic activities tied in with the natural geographic features and physical resources of the community? To what degree are there seasonal and cyclical fluctuations in employment? How do other activities and resources in the region affect the economic life of the community?

In what areas are there seasonal changes in employment? What have been the trends in employment during the past ten years? How do these compare with other communities in the area and in the state? Are there changes in industry and in the economic picture which may require retraining of workers? Are new industries making demands for different skills? Is there an increase in leisure time, due either to shorter hours or increased unemployment? How strong are labor unions, and in which industries? What is their place in the community? Are they accepted and active in the community affairs, or are they isolated? Do union members belong to other organizations, or are their activities limited to those of the unions? Are the predominant occupations those in which employees are dependent for job advancement on self-improvement?

What kinds of manufactures are most heavily represented? What is the total value added by manufacture and how does it compare with similar communities in the state? In which are the most people employed? What kinds of businesses, and particularly, what kinds of services are provided? What enterprises employ the most people? What kinds of retail stores are most heavily represented? What is their volume of business? What goods and services have to be obtained out-

side the community? How does the library create and utilize contacts
with business and industry to increase their knowledge of library resources and programs?

Educational Life

What is the educational level of the various groupings in the population? Are there adequate buildings, materials and personnel? To
what degree do adults of the community participate in the educational
activities? What kinds of formal and informal opportunities are provided to meet the needs and interests of the total population?

What are the local sources for resource materials? What can be
learned about community tastes and interests from TV, radio, and newspapers? What can the local bookstore tell about local communication
interests and ability? What light does the library circulation and requests for material and information throw on this? Is there any one
source of information on what is available?

What educational opportunities are available in the community, both
formal and informal? What action is being taken to coordinate educational
activities in the community? Is there eigher formal or informal cooperation in planning and presenting educational programs? Do the subjects
offered, level and method of presentation, location and time of activity,
give a range of choice for all elements in the community? Are educational
programs provided by industry? By labor unions? By business and
service enterprises? What educational opportunities are available in
the surrounding area? What are the characteristics of the educational
methodologies, testing facilities, special programs, teacher competencies
and administrative policies?

Cultural Life

What are the cultural opportunities in the community? Who makes
use of these opportunities? Are there people interested in some activities
that the community does not provide? What are the commonly held attitudes, prejudices and customs which influence activities in the community and which may cause the isolation of various groups? Are these attitudes held from the past or formed from new and changing conditions?
What minority groups are well integrated into the community in housing?
Church membership? School attendance? Community organizations?

What is the character of family life in the community? Do people
tend to take part in activities as families. Does each member have his
own circle or interest group? What is the proportion of broken homes?
Of working mothers? What are the community's religious characteristics? Which denominations are most predominant? How well are the
churches supported? What role do churches play in the community?
Are they centers for social life? What kinds of programs do church
groups offer?

What programs do museums, art galleries, musical groups, concerns,
handcraft groups offer, and what are the costs and conditions under
which the individual may take part? What is the quality and coverage
of local radio and TV programs? How much of the programming is educational in purpose? By what means are audio-visual resources coordinated for maximum use in the community? What kinds of recreation are
available in the area? What groups in the community do they serve?
What other library resources are available in the area? In the state?

Public Services

What are the standards of housing? Is there community planning,
for such items as transportations, traffic, water and sanitation? Are
the services of the health and welfare departments available to all citizens? Do all citizens know of their services? Are these activities
coordinated to any degree? What can be learned about the local level
of living?

What does the census tell about the characteristics of housing?
What proportion of dwellings are single-unit? multiple unit? What is
the average number of persons per unit? per room? What proportion
of dwellings are owner-occupied? What is the median rental per month?
What proportion of dwellings are unoccupied?

Local Government

What are the qualifications of candidates for public office? What
is the degree of interest and concern on the part of all citizens in governmental activities? Is the spirit of the community cooperative,
friendly, alert, realistically optimistic? Are citizens interested and
do they participate in activities to improve the community? Is there
skilled and experienced leadership available?

What is the character and caliber of local government? Are there
standards of community service in education, protection, welfare,

sanitation, highways? Is it a "well-kept" town? Is it static or progressive? Is it planning ahead, or meeting needs as they arise? What groups assume citizen responsibility? Who are the people that influence decisions and the acceptance of new ideas and action in the community? What kinds of positions do they hold?

Resources

Are there adequate and appropriate resources to meet community needs? Are the citizens aware of resources available to them in the region and the state? How well are these resources used? Are there problems of communication among the agency and institution resources? Are there problems in coordinating plans and activities? How many of the leaders in community organizations know and use the library as individuals? Are they from only one segment of the population or do they represent a cross-section?

What is the character of community organizational activity? What means are there for coordinating and integrating community activities? Does a community calendar exist, and who is responsible for keeping it up? How is community leadership being developed? Who provides program planning institutes and leadership training? How many and which organizations have educational and/or community development objectives? Is this information readily available, and where? Can these programs be improved, increased, and extended? How general is participation in community organizational activities? How many organizations are open to all who wish to join?

CITIZEN INVOLVEMENT AND DEVELOPMENT

The central purpose of community development is educational in focus and realized through the involvement of an ever increasing number of citizens. This is especially the objective to be kept in mind with the technique of community study where the temptation may be strong to get the survey done as quickly and "efficiently" as possible. But such a procedure misses the essential point that community study is an educational method and is not designed as a rigorous research proposal.

Community development as a communicative method together with its associated study design is employed in order to involve volunteers in continuing and self educational activities. The professional staff must undertake widespread and continuous recruitment and sponsor group work programs of a high order of communicative effectiveness. Locating and recruiting participants who can be trained for and involved in leadership development may include the following techniques:

Personal contacts (over-the-desk, interviews, over-the telephone)

Notices (in church bulletins, descriptive notes in pay envelopes)

Personal appearances (labor groups, civic organizations)

Mailings (alumni lists, voting lists)

Recruiting can never be a mass enterprise. Its activities are highly specialized, and much attention must be given to detail. Each recruit is an individual and must be treated as someone having important differences from every other person. Names of potential recruits simply as names are practically worthless. Other pertinent facts must be discovered: age, economic background, special interests, abilities and skills, memberships in organizations, activities in the community, friends and business associates, political affiliations, occupation. The following questions may prove helpful in considering the development of a volunteer recruitment program:

What happens to the people who have joined an organization? Can they become active members or sit back and wait for other people to run the show? Do they maintain their original interest in the organization or after the initial enthusiasm has worn away, do their attendence and participation slack off? Do they find the personal satisfaction they were promised or are they disappointed? Do they find more, or less, than they expected when they volunteered to become involved?

Personal contact is the best approach. Names of potential members should be parceled out on the basis of related interests. No method has ever been more effective than a face-to-face one. Personal conviction about involvement in community development work is evident in the tone of voice, facial expression, or choice of words. The sales talk can be personally adapted to the response of the prospect. The volunteer can be moved to immediate action. Telephone a potential recruit and ask for a personal interview.

If a personal contact is impossible, there are other methods of approach. The prospective volunteer can be invited to one or several meetings. If possible, call up and ask him to attend with you personally. When he arrives at the meeting, see that he meets many others and that he has a pleasant impression of the agency and its community development work. If possible, familiarize the prospect with other types of activity in the organization. Always be sensitive to the feelings of the person you are trying to attract. Know his interests, likes and dislikes, friends and foes, and act accordingly.

Send the prospective volunteer leaflets or publications which will interest him and that tell him about the agency and its activities. Do not send him too much — just enough to intrigue and make him want more. If he must be invited into participation by a personal letter, see that it is signed by someone favorably known to him or by someone whose invitation carries weight with him. In addition there should always be a personal follow-up by telephone or an invitation to a specific meeting for a particular purpose.

All staff members need to work together to see that every volunteer remains interested in community organization and active in its work. An up-to-date census of individual volunteers should be maintained by keeping: (a) data of members' activities, interest, time on a membership card; (b) up-do-date records of participation; (c) semi-annual interviews with individual members. A personal interview with individual volunteers makes possible continuous feedback on the possibilities for participation as recruits are interested in doing. Such a developmental interview checks dissatisfactions, and gives the volunteer a feeling that he is important to the organization of community enterprise:

What things about the agency and its program have you found to be good and useful to you?

What kind of work, other than what you have done in the past, would you like to become involved with?

Do you feel that there are any things you would like to do that you've found impossible to do thus far?

Are there any differences between what you expected to find as a recruit and what you have actually found?

Within the agency, do you have any pet peeves you would like to see corrected?

What one thing in the agency do you consider to be most in
need of modification?

Compared with other agencies or organizations in which you
have been a member, how do you feel about this one?

In addition to evaluation, the goals of each work group must be kept
constantly in review and opportunities created so that volunteers will
be able to participate in the widest range of activities and positions as
possible. It is better to keep each group small, almost a cell, rather
than to risk the loss of a member through under involvement. The following points may be kept in mind when meeting the problems of maintaining group activity:

Provide many opportunities for participation.
    Planning programs.
    Doing special jobs.
    Working on committees.
    Making reports (even though not a chairman).
    Small group discussion.

Provide opportunities for developing skills.
    Discussion techniques.
    Group participation.
    Public speaking.

Relate policy and program to member needs.
    Wide opportunity for participation.
    Dues within members reach.
    Money raising not too burdensome.
    Effective committee structure.
    Democratic election procedure.

Review organizational activities.
    Small group meetings of total membership.

Recognize member contributions
    Local news reports.
    House organs.
    General meetings.
    Involve in responsibilities.

It is impossible to meet human needs without working with other
people. The communicator must articulate his efforts into a series of

programs with specific goals of time, money and resources if he is to avoid the routine and mediocre. The participants must learn to separate out the routine and take care of it quickly, efficiently and accurately. In order to analyze any problem, adequate representation is needed from all segments of the community whether professional, political or the lay citizenry.

Work groups have to be assembled around various interests and tasks. Study and work groups will analyze problems, gather data, and propose possible solutions. The decision will also be taken as to how the work can be broken down and who will be responsible for carrying through the entire program. The program director can be made responsible for dividing the work into task areas, for assigning specialists to see that the necessary tasks are completed, and for providing a working relationship so that the volunteers' and other participants' contributions can be integrated.

The feasibility of any idea or community development activity has to be worked out within significant constraints. Group development work determines whether an idea has any contribution to offer in meeting human needs. Group work is a fundamental method for study and decision making in the community enterprise. Group members must know how or be taught to participate in group action. The professional communicator helps volunteers and various staff members progress in this self-development as the program unfolds. As a result staff and volunteers should be able in time to exert leadership and help others to perform. The ability of group members to work effectively towards a shared goal is the real basis for success.

Adequate Group	Inadequate Group
Group work units generally on time and within budget, or policy	Members habitually behind on group assigned tasks.
Participants busy but give impression of having program under control.	Always rushed and find it difficult to meet deadlines.
Necessary changes and redirection made in a timely way and taken in stride.	Changes are radical, made too late and often with traumatic consequences.

Adequate Group	Inadequate Group
Each member growing fast in experience, and in readiness for bigger assignments.	Group members feel frustrated and stagnant and complain about learning little.

Group meetings constitute one of the best techniques for coordinating the work of various individuals. Merely going through the motions of coordination will not suffice. All members and especially the communicator must ensure that human interface problems are identified and resolved. Data confrontation will not solve human difficulties. Nor on the other hand will group sensitivity sessions necessarily hold the continuing attention of busy recruits who have volunteered to "lend a hand" to the development of agency-community relations.

No communicative change agent can work effectively without extensive sensitivity training on his own part. However, in the daily give-and-take of community endeavor, his actual working role is a feedback facilitator to offset the interpersonal problems which his "third ear" tells him may be developing. Continuous feedback will indicate which tasks should be augumented and which decreased or modified so that the program can run smoothly and efficiently. Each participant must learn and promote the conditions which constitute effective group action:

The current status of the program, its specifications, changes and information about the person(s) for whom it is being designed are made available to all members as rapidly as possible.

Frequent meetings are held to review progress or the lack of it in the program as a whole and the work of individuals. Interface problems can be identified and quickly resolved.

All participants work to make meetings productive by digging into presentations to get at the meat of situations and problems. This objective is accomplished when participants:

Suppress discussion which has little bearing on the work at hand or to its related aspects.

Investigate the possibility of alternative solutions even if apparently unfavorable to their own concerns.

Stand ready to present at any time briefly, clearly and impersonally the status and problems of their own work.

Identify the work of other participants and as promptly
give credit for it as they are to accept credit for
their own contributions.

All members, but especially the program leader write the
specifications for each area of responsibility and each interface as soon as possible.

Each participant can receive without delay minutes of any
program meeting. Included in these memoranda are
brief summaries of problems discussed, major events
that have occurred, and especially decisions and assignments
made at the meeting.

Each member keeps his own time commitments. However
when it is impossible to do so, the individual will inform his
project and other involved participants as far ahead as possible.

Project members must follow the work of each other closely enough
to understand how each task fits into the whole pattern, despite the im-
mature feeling that this might be meddling. Where subsystem interface
is involved, each member must know enough to observe specifications
and previous agreements. Members cannot expect the program leader
to define work assignments specifically nor oversee every piece of work
and how it fits into program requirements. The librarian encourages
discussion of ideas by the whole team, not just in two-man relationships
with each member individually.

AGENCY CONTROL

Effective control in library organization includes scheduling, monitoring, controlling. Control directs a program so that goals may be
accomplished within time and money schedules. Control is maintained
during the entire project. Scheduling is that part of control which includes planning and recording. With the help of group members, the
leader analyzes and develops the tasks to be accomplished:

Establish initial concept or problem.

Determine critical factors in each area of concern.

Specify all interface conditions and alternatives.

Establish estimates for attainable specifications.

Establish final configuration and make recommendations.

Complete proposed program protocol together with costs
for distribution to the policy making groups.

Each of these tasks should have a completion target. Critical factors
to be determined in each area of the program should be placed in the
supervising coordinator's hands. Interface boundary specifications must
be identified and agreed to by each project group in the coordinated enterprise. Decisions made in each meeting are accepted by consensus of
all members. Program meeting memoranda together with the overall
schedules become specific guidelines for each participant. Once the
total configuration of the community development project is completed,
it becomes a brief orientation document to the various components of
the enterprise:

Schedule the whole project at the beginning, and recognize
the interdependence of various parts.

Identify the critical items early, and update a current list
of them.

Seek out the best time and cost estimates available for
critical items.

Modify and update work project schedules as needed.

Bring all contributors, or contributing groups into the
scheduling process.

Communication is essential at all stages of project work, especially
at its termination when the information developed by the project is stored
in a report or model, or a design. Paper work is an indispensable tool
for both factual and aesthetic (emotional) considerations. People do not
live by facts alone and need the emotionally supportive and coordinating
influence of interval reports on progress. Report writing and dissemination is an important component in the community development enterprise.
The elements of effective report writing include the following:

Conclusions stated clearly and specifically constitute
the essential structure of the report.

Information which backs up the conclusions and is carefully keyed to each of them enables the reader to judge
for himself how valid the conclusions are.

Procedures and conditions (assumptions and methods)
should be so carefully indicated that someone unknown
to the project team could repeat the work with similar
results.

A summary, table of contents and headings not only
articulate the separation of parts but also make the
report quick and easy to use.

Pictures, drawings and charts are most helpful when
keyed carefully to the text and the text to them. Appendices can be used for the bulk of data and backup
material. Ideally the main body of a report should
be relatively short with references to more extensive
material in appendices.

In whatever way the progress of the project is summarized for presentation, some conceptual framework is required in order to communicate precisely the generalizations, the supporting data and proposed
solutions. The frame of reference within which the report is embedded
is of course, in general, the situation-producing theory of a communicative profession that provides a guide to the significant aspects of patron
interface and the backup infrastructure. Based upon concepts such as
these, the criteria for excellence in report writing appear to include the
following:

Completeness in the report answers questions about
accomplishments, or lack of them and especially with
respect to which project goals and claims are backed
up with evidence.

The report is as simple as possible, consistent with the
fact that the report stands for the project. Clarity and
organization are indispensable.

Technical correctness implies that the project reflects
the work done.

When time and money are invested in a project, a report
received in time provides a base for decision-making.

More specifically, community development project work is undertaken within the framework of control documents of a particular agency
or organization. At the outset it is important to state the broad objectives
of the proposed agency program in relation to its community or the institution or organization of which it is a part. Such an undertaking will
help to answer the question of why an informational and educational service is needed at all as well as what characteristics of the users it will
satisfy. The development of any type of agency service should be ex-
plored in relation to the extent of cooperative activity with other communication centers in the community, state and nation. Cooperation should
have a beneficial effect on all the possible products of the informational
and educational services used by the public(s).

Some consideration should be given before policies are written as
to the kinds of services which might be offered and how these services
are related to the characteristics of the various user groups. Policies
constitute the general method by which the professional staff interface
with the user public. Policy includes the best professional expertise
subordinate to community and user needs. Through policy, the patron
enters the system and by means of professional expertise is taken to
any other point in the system he may wish to go. Since policies are
carried out by professional staff, it is important to the personnel who
are to assume responsibility for the services. Ways and means should
be considered whereby other informational and infrastructure services'
staff can be kept informed of concerns in the community, program plans
and changes, or data collection and interpretation activities of specialists
and citizen volunteers.

Few attempts have been made to lay out the service aspects of the
informational and educational agency in a way that is functionally iso-
morphic with human development. What study there has been on the
maturation process of the self-actualizing individual has not frequently
been employed in the diagnosis of information needs and development.
The same careful analysis of steps which have taken place in the flow-
chart school of reference work should be applied to other developmental
needs of the individual whether for counseling, guidance, group work or
community development.

The process of continuous evaluation and feedback is probably the
best way to expedite orderly change. Everyone concerned with the informational and educational service, including citizens, should be involved in evaluation. Self-appraisal includes both those who provide
the services as well as the actual and potential patrons. Comparison
of achievement with objectives within a program leads to more growth
than comparison of one program with another.

The service public(s) actually does evaluate programs sometimes directly and other times through elected officials. Evaluation should be more concerned with results than with energy spent and objectives should recede as they are approached. Circulation, hours open, money spent may account for time and energy, but in themselves reveal little evidence of changes wrought in behavior. The evaluation of services is concerned with outcomes, i. e., results and changes in people in answer to the question: What difference does this activity make?

Coordinated resource center services can be more effective in promoting an interface between the general public and all the information sources in a community. Leadership administration should be concerned about the methods of communication in its various contexts rather than information acquisition. Management administration should be subordinate to leadership administration whose major concerns are with market analysis studies and content analysis studies. Subsequent findings will be used to establish the specifications for information control devices. The communications staff have ultimate responsibility for all decisions as to information control methods in order to create situations within which communication (information surprise) can occur.

SIX

COMMUNITY AS AN EDUCATIONAL FORCE

Community study may serve as a field research project but of greater significance is the fact that it is a major educational and communicative method for involving activists and others in studying the need for, and significance of community change. Ways for identifying educational and information needs and interests are indicated as well as resources which will make it possible for the resource center to meet its imperatives as a coordinating structure in the community. Of equal or perhaps greater significance are the methods for involving an ever increasing number of individuals in studying the need for change. Only by educational methods such as these can people in a democracy be expected to bring about any effective and lasting developments for the betterment of community life.

The community is both a lab and a matrix of interactions within which informational and educational messages or programs are designed to meet specific needs and interests of particular audiences. Integrated media, library, and information service has a responsibility for developing its own informational and educational programs and for serving as a coordinating structure within the community. In principle, library-like services should not be fragmented: steps whose aims are to meet standards are now underway in order to overcome the limitations of type of library service. As media, library and information centers merge or, possibly, federate into systems in increased numbers, more programs of an integrated nature aimed at the community as a whole will be developed for a wider range of communities.

The resource specialist who subscribes to community development and betterment usually undertakes some aspects of community study in order to open up and to widen the range of opportunities for individuals to participate in community activities and to make it possible for significantly greater numbers of people to have a voice in policy determination. In its initial stages of implementation and development, community study begins as a survey research technique for the identification of various community informational needs, interests, problems, and resources.

Of course, data is gathered which supports findings in these areas, but the citizens in ever widening numbers soon find themselves involved in questions of interpretation of the data and the implications of the findings for the resource center and other agencies of the community. This implies that citizens are regarded as more than respondents to questionnaires and interviews. Citizens are involved in asking as well as answering questions, in collecting as well as providing data, and in sending as well as receiving messages. The very process of study and interpretation becomes the matrix for innumerable individual informational and educational learning experiences.

When people know the facts, even though controversial, and especially when they are involved in data identification they are more apt to make a better life for themselves. These facts can be learned most effectively by professionals and other community leaders through continuous community survey. Programming as well as information dissemination bring facts to community awareness so that individuals with a multiplicity of interests can study together in work groups and eventually develop action programs. Librarians generally either have yet to realize that controversial issues have unparalleled priority in motivating people to participate or are afraid to become involved in such issues.

The formula "Who need to know what?" is taken as the prototype of the various questions asked in the process of interpretation. On the surface and in the beginning it looks relatively simple but very soon the activities implied by the interpreted data take on dimensions that were only latent in the initial, and what soon appears to be a global formulation of the question. Volunteers and professionals are suddenly plunged into the whole area of communications and, in particular, into those two concerns which lie at the heart of communicative services to the public: audience research and content analysis.

Community concerns and the interests of various publics usually become evident when the question, "Who needs to know what?" is asked about each of the findings in a community study. "Who?" may be answered in a number of ways: the general public, a defined group in the population, people responsible for action, such as government, agency or institutional officers, organization leaders, key people. More than one such category will usually be listed in response to the question of "Who" as well as in response to "What." The answers to "What" fall into several categories: the factors and implications in the situation (information and understanding); knowledge of accepted practice in dealing with it; adequacy of present resources; availability of state and national resources; experiences of other communities in dealing with a similar concern; and how the "what" can be utilized by the "whos."

In the past, librarians have been fairly circumspect in their response to community issues. They have been largely content to provide materials to meet demands and, where controversy has emerged, have struggled to preserve their dignity about intellectual freedom. In a few instances, there have been some attempts toward program development which have been known as adult education. However, in order to satisfy those citizens of a more Machiavellian turn of mind as well as meet pragmatic questions of vested interest, program negotiation cannot be ignored.

As a basis for program planning, the coordinator and participants should gather all possible facts through existing community agencies or other types of local resources which relate to group wants, needs, and interests. In order to be effective, program development has to center on controversy and activism as the core of its planning. Facts refer to attitudes and feelings as well as the quantitative data that traditionally has played a dominant role. It is the attitudes and feelings of citizens which make facts; it is their reality that makes a community what it is and in many cases not what it appears to be.

Communicators have long ago taken the position that controversy and anxiety pave the road to active participation and crucial learning for the vast majority of people in any community. Such an orientation may be anxiety-producing for the average librarian, but there are a number of steps which can be taken in planning effective programs:

> Analyze your own resources as a program coordinator as well as the resources and equipment of group members and of the community.

> Inform yourself and the group about the real conditions surrounding the general content of a proposed program. If it deals, for example, with city government, visit the various departments, read and collect all available materials. Sample the attitudes and feelings of the employees and administrators.

> Consult specialists and resource persons who are familiar with pertinent activities and materials in the program under consideration. Find out how other groups have carried on a particular type of program by means of visits to such community agencies and groups.

Area of Problem or Concern	Who? needs to know	What?
Lack of appreciation for continuing education and facilities for it -- also related sub-topics	Staff and boards of agencies	1. The problem 2. Needs and interests of public as determined by community study 3. Principles and techniques of communication with public at all economic, social, and educational levels 4. Methods of coordinating efforts 5. Ways to assess costs and to meet them 6. Existing or potential resources
	Leaders of organizations	1. The problem 2. Program content and methods to stimulate interest and appreciation of members themselves, and to stimulate them to community action
Lack of overall planning for a fast growing mobile community -- also related sub-topics	Leaders of the Community	1. The problem 2. How other communities deal with it 3. Principles of effective community action 4. What state, national, local resources are available

Assemble all available materials such as books,
documents, charts, maps, that may provide solutions
to problems arising in the program, using group members to aid in this work as far as possible. Make the
activities and experiences in a program as concrete as
possible using illustrative materials: pictures, dia-
grams, charts, scrapbooks, posters.

Have your group elect small committees which can
better aid in planning the detail of the work in a unit
of the program series. Any unit in the series should
remain flexible enough to permit adaptations to meet
interests and needs as they arise.

The resource center can often make its greatest potential contribution
to the community by providing increased services for people, particularly
in imaginative training for citizenship. The resource center has an obligation to mobilize all of its own resources as well as other resources
in the community in order to help people get all the information necessary
with which to make intelligent decisions and lead more enlightened lives.
In order to do this, the library must be involved in a planned way in as
many community activities as possible. Of course, planning and the
setting of priorities are essential, otherwise librarians will run the risk
of becoming all things to all people. As the major force serving as a
coordinating structure in the community, the resource center will achieve
maximum results from a continuing survey.

Of the two principal functions of a social agency, recreation and education, the first is relatively easy to perform. Providing people with
satisfying recreation for their leisure hours involves no great difficulty
for the experience professional. It is, however, more difficult to serve
social and educational needs especially when these are controversial and
do not fit the neat categories of intellectual freedom which are so fashion-
able today. The library has so often been called a multipurpose agency
that one may well wonder whether this may be its essential weakness.
Community study, with its complexity in terms of patrons, resources,
and objectives has forced an awareness on librarians of the complexity
of the problems. Needs for self-education are extremely heterogeneous.
Varied approaches and educational techniques are needed.

In addition to the traditional informational and educational services
expected from libraries, other responsibilities are added by community
study. By involving an increasingly wider range of adults in community

study, the librarian is determining subject areas in which the library and
other community agencies can prepare "units" of program development
for "curricular" study. The immediate program planning of agencies,
organizations and groups shifts in accordance with the progressive, cooperative identification of community problems and interests.

AVENUES OF CHANGE

Although uncertainties exist in the minds of a few librarians, community development and its educational method will help them create an
educative environment and meet their responsibility for actively promoting
the liberal self-education of all adults. In so doing, the social objectives
of the library can become more explicit. It is obvious that the task of
providing resources and creating educational situations for all adults is
a task beyond the ability of any single agency or institution.

The basic educational problem is one of helping people see that a
broadening of community involvement is more important than an increased
educative load for any one agency. To the extent that librarians grow in
their commitment to life-long and life-wide self-education of themselves,
the library will begin to emerge as a community learning center in educational methods and techniques which can be applied in meeting a variety of interests. The library is no longer just an agency; it has become
a method for aiding people to learn continuously.

With community study, librarians begin to accept the necessity for
utilizing in program development not only the resources of the community but the experiences of various members in the community. People
who do not readily take to "adult education" may respond better to indigenous community development projects. A community related library
can promote an improved community-wide background. People learn
better and faster when the knowledge sought is chosely related to everyday activities in the community. This is evident in the fact that the programming of television networks is beginning to have almost as potent
an influence on the citizen as his actual community background.

Proof of the effectiveness of community study is in the changes, real
and intangible, which can take place in the library staff and staff development is an important consideration of the floating librarian. To some
extent, librarians become self-conscious, looking at themselves critically
and objectively. They begin to consider the community more broadly
and factually, developing a sense of involvement in and responsibility
for the community's problems and needs. Recognizing their adult liberal

education responsibility to the community, librarians also begin the slow process of making it difficult for the majority of people to avoid thinking about the issues in the community and in the world at large. By so doing, the floating librarian may enrich and embody in human terms for all people the myth of intellectual freedom which is now in many instances only championed for the few who make noises.

An immediate achievement which the community librarian finds invaluable is discussion group training. Experience in discussion groups will not only improve individual reader guidance, but it will give librarian confidence to sit down in groups and explore community problems. Of course, librarians have long recognized the importance of identifying an individual's reason for seeking information. But with discussion group experience they begin to understand how group goals are developed and adopted by the entire group, not a strident advocating minority. In such a way the group dramatically starts where its members are, not where the advocate or the librarian previously may have thought they should be. With community study, librarians also learn that thinking and discussion should lead to a desire to do something about the situation discussed and to formulate a plan for action.

In searching for a rationalization why such a study might be undertaken, librarians are led to the point where community involvement must be justified in terms of their social objectives. The challenges are stimulating and so much is involved that it is unnecessary to accept a community development approach merely because it has proved successful elsewhere. The first steps may seem disturbing and traumatic. What is an objective? Is there a relationship between an objective and method? What is it?

These and many other questions challenge librarians and trustees to think, write out a statement of social objectives and determine methods and policies through which the library staff and citizens' group can help implement these objectives. The change agent seeks to identify and use community interests and problems for the growth and development of people in the community. A librarian can identify groups (the who's) that can use information (the what's) for a community-oriented library service program. Consequently community development involves social processes such as the following:

> Community identity: As people become more conscious of their own community, they become more closely identified with the community area in which

they live and function. They understand how their
community differs from others, and also realize
how similar their community is to others.

Meeting unmet needs or solving problems: Organized
communities appear to have more problems than unorganized ones, because organized communities simply
recognize more of their problems. The determination
of community needs by the people themselves and the
recognition of these problems is the first step in the
process. These will be recognized as common problems
and collective action is required to solve them. People
learn how to deal with conflict and utilize it to produce
real solutions to problems which are better than simple
compromise.

Fuller social participation: People cannot develop their
talents, personalities, and resources, unless they
participate in groups. The coordinating structure especially, provides the opportunity to expand social participation. The structure may be used to promote participation in existing organizations and programs or it
may be used to create new organizational structures.
One expression of this process is the fact that people
who actively participate in a number of organizations
are much more likely to request the services of floating
librarians than those with a lower level of participation.

Obtaining social control: In the main, individuals and
specific groups conform to community standards, ideals,
and goals. It is logical to assume that a large proportion
of the people will support a coordinating structure if it
is their program and if it is meeting their needs and
solving their problems. Effective social control, therefore, involves the development of a high degree of community loyalty or community esprit de corps.

Coordinating groups and activities: In almost any community, several organizations attempt to carry out the
same or very similar types of programs. There is a
continuous need for unifying efforts: it saves time,
money, and leadership resources. All the organizations
in the community which are involved in promoting any

program might pool their efforts and serve the community much better. Many types of community problems
cannot be solved by even a whole community working
alone. Some problems require the combined efforts of
two or more communities as well as working with outside organizations and agencies.

Developing community leaders: If a community is to
act, it must have leadership. Leadership by definition
develops only through group situations. There is no
such thing as leadership outside of a group context.
Every community has some type of leadership and every
normal individual has leadership capacity under certain
conditions. Every community, if it is to develop and make
progress, must have leaders who see the whole community. Leadership capabilities can be discovered and further
developed by giving adults in a community a job in relation
to their capabilities, and by giving young people places of
responsibility in their own community.

Community floating librarians have found the community study method
invaluable not only in motivating community action but also in channeling
the exuberance of activists into productive enterprises. As discussion,
or rather argument proceeds, negotiation may occur and out of the bargaining grows a new proposal. In any event, the following questions may
prove useful in establishing priorities among community concerns:

What is the significance of the concern to the community?
Is it really vital? What is the relationship of concerns
and problems to each other?

Does it affect the total community or only a segment of
the population? With whom should the resource agency
work for outside resources and for cooperation?

Is this a long or short term problem? If short term,
are there more serious, underlying, intangible factors?

Who is doing something about it? Who is aware of it?
What understanding is there? action? apathy? re-
sistance to it? or resources for meeting it in the community?

Which concern will be easiest for the resource agency to
deal with? Which is most difficult? Which one needs an
immediate solution?

AGENCY REVIEW

Once librarians have taken a thoughtful look at themselves in the
light of social objectives, they find that they need the community almost
more than the community needs them. Community resources increase
in value as aids in finding a solution for problems. Community enterprise becomes an experience furnished with such educational elements
as motivation, problems in a life situation, group thinking and other
socializing procedures and the actual trying out of proposed solutions
followed by evaluation. The worth of professional learning has been
checked against an increasing ability and skill in meeting individual
and community problems. It is especially important that staff thoroughly
understand the educational role of the agency in whatever they decide
to do:

What are the actual and potential resource backgrounds
of the staff? What special abilities do members of the
staff possess?

What changes need to be made in:

Staff responsibilities
Materials and purchasing policies
Staff attitudes toward the community and various groups?
The approach to extended services
Developing and focusing publicity
Staff willingness to take on new responsibilities and try
out new techniques

Can you make a decision on what to do in one or more of
the problem areas? How can you evaluate what you do in
terms of objectives?

Based upon study findings, the staff develops a confidence to take
a courageous and imaginative approach. With limited staff and funds,
the agency may have to set priorities. Its public relations program can
begin to move in the direction of making educational pursuits attractive.
The image of the media center which it keeps before the public should
be one of a place where all people can educate themselves continuously.

Since it is an educational institution, not merely a book and information
dispensing station, the communication center becomes concerned about
issues in addition to mere publicity for the agency. Adults have been
asked not only to help identify desirable avenues for social changes but
also invited to help the resource center plan its services in that direction.

The media center staff and trustees need not feel that they stand
alone in developing educational services to meet needs. They can call
on members of the former Citizen's Committee and many other volunteers. The following questions can be used as a guide to (1) help plan
an activity (reminder of essential elements), (2) report an activity to
trustees, the public or the profession, (3) evaluate an activity as a base-
line or statement of intentions to be reviewed at intervals or at the end
of the activity:

What is the educational objective of this activity?

Which of the findings of the study prompted it?

What specific agency goal does it meet?

How does it involve message space?

How does it involve community resources?
(in planning and execution)

What segments of the community does it serve?
How will it affect other programs, agencies and
organizations?

How will it be evaluated and what plans have been
made to continue it or to build on it?

The organizational structure must develop goals and methods of
procedure which are acceptable to the people. The goals of a coordinating structure can be developed out of the actual needs of the community. These goals, to be understood, must provide a strong motivating
force for people to join together to meet common needs. The general
methods and procedures must be acceptable to the people and should be
worked out from the goals of the particular community. These goals
must be widely understood by all the people in order to avoid the tendency
among many communities for the goals to be placed in the background.
In such instances, the particular action projects will become ends in
themselves and not the educational enterprise which must be carried on
continuously in every organized community.

In studying the community and in interpreting findings, the community coordinator must seek the aid of other individuals and groups. Advisory committees and study groups can render valuable assistance in gathering information about the community and in helping to interpret it for the program development. The communicator also utilizes community study in an educational and communications process. Such a teaching method provides opportunities for individual self-improvement, and arouses citizen interest in social action and improved community living. Among the many activities which can be undertaken in program development, the following may serve as examples:

Locate appropriate materials for purchase or to borrow; create new materials to meet the specific need of the group.

Adjust the agency's publicity program for special emphasis on topics and recommendations resulting from the needs not being met by the various components of the coordinating council.

Confer with all other resource specialists in the community — public, school, college, university, hospital, institutional, special — to insure availability of all resources and cooperative planning of activities.

Confer with other agencies in the community for local activities planned, meeting of the committees, study programs, publicity programs; key people—delegates, committee members, subject specialists; kinds of materials and services likely to be needed; areas of library-agency cooperation.

Organize information on community activities and resources of special importance to community development; calendar of meetings; Program resource file—speakers, penal members, films, charts, materials from other agencies.

Bulletin boards and exhibits for special information; develop reading lists and other resource leaflets on appropriate topics.

Publicize the availability of such information; provide other resource leaflets on appropriate topics.

Prepare a collection of materials of particular use to clubs and organizations with special interest to their involvement with the community's concerns and interests.

Inform club presidents and program chairmen of availability and use of such materials for programs, committee work and study; mail an informative brochure; call a meeting in the media center to introduce materials and demonstrate their use.

Invite delegates and local committee members to visit the media center in order to examine materials and discuss services either individually or at a designated time for the entire group.

Use the agency's usual newspaper space or radio or TV time to provide information on community development; ask key people to take part in programs—before and after the community development project; offer time and space to appropriate agencies; review materials and show films on significant topics.

Sponsor or cosponsor with other agencies and organizations: meetings, discussion series, audiovisual programs on community development; adjust leadership training and program planning clinics to prevailing concerns.

Institute a training program for hard-core unemployed in service areas; provide a program for completion of high school; provide counseling services to community members; develop a CCC type program organizing community members to clean up and paint the community.

Organize a community communications program; set up a common newspaper publicizing group efforts; establish a TV and radio station; identify group or community leaders and have them work at the chairmanship level of these committees.

Initiate a political power and legal base from which to operate; set up system of ward or sectional chairmen to pool political resources of each section; hold monthly meetings to discuss political thrusts; initiate write-in (mass type) compaigns to force an awareness of issues beneficial to this community.

Train resource "Vista" aides in groups and as individuals in a program of new careers in libraries for the poor; persons indigenous to the neighborhoods can develop professional and language skills needed for the promotion and exploitation of relevant materials.

Develop coffee house programs cooperatively with other
helping agencies in order to provide materials, classes,
retraining programs, staff and, advisory services; home
visits by resource "Vista" aides with inexpensive materials
of family and individual interests; working kits of materials
custom designed can be left by "Vista" aides.

In order to nourish the development of a structure through which
the community is to be changed, people must become discontented with
existing conditions in their community. This involves the development
of an image of potentiality or maturity not only among leaders but as
widespread as possible among all the people. Librarians must develop
the image of potentiality in terms of physical resources and in terms
of development of each of the major institutional areas. However it is
the people themselves and their total potentiality which must be recruited.
It is the responsibility of resource specialists as community leaders to
help develop this discontent and to inculcate the development of an image
of potentiality and maturity.

The discontent generated must be focused and channeled into organization. The professional staff must undertake the task of studying the
particular community and of understanding its problems. Communications
involves planning in order to meet unmet needs and to develop human
potentiality. But it also involves an action program, a program designed
step by step to develop the potentialities in the community, as well as
human and natural resources. The problems of the community are not
insurmountable provided resource specialists employ organizational
structure, the proper procedure, and a fundamental action program
through which these specific problems can be solved.

The organizational structure should involve all the leaders in the
community. There are leaders in formal positions in the various organizations in the community. However much of the leadership is what
is sometimes called the informal type—that is, they do not function
through formal positions of leadership, rather they are sometimes called
the power behind the scene. These earned leaders must be identified
and accepted by the librarian's organizational structure.

Each of the major subgroups in the community, whether formal or
informal, has some people in it who influence the behavior of others.
These leaders must be identified and involved so as to obtain their assistance in the agency's development program. Sometimes the expression
is heard that, "This community has no leadership." But what is meant

is that the available leadership is not acceptable to persons making such statements. Communicators reach out and make contact so as to bring all subgroups into the framework of community development.

SERVICE TO PUBLICS

There is an important distinction to be made between service to publics and group dynamics. Group dynamics is the term for the process in which a small highly interactive group is involved (109). The group meets regularly over a period of time in order to consider some need or interest of the participants, establish its purposes, and achieve some behavioral outcomes. On the other hand, service to a public is essentially program planning for an audience of any size which is largely noninteractive. The programs planned may be sequential and if there are as few as three programs in a series on one theme, then the sequence can be considered to be educational in the broad sense.

Service to publics considers large segments of the population as a whole which can be identified fairly clearly by demographic, socioeconomic, attitudinal, and cultural characteristics, such as labor, disadvantaged, aged. Once identified, their characteristics have to be transformed into educational and information needs. Then and only then is it possible to ask the seminal question underlying all program development: WHO needs to know WHAT about the aspects of these topics? The steps in the procedure may include the following:

List the characteristics of that segment of the population about which you are concerned.

Restate these characteristics as informational and educational needs or interests.

Who besides your population segment also needs to know about the needs and interests of your segment of the population.

What does each of these other segments need to know about your segment of the population.

When, where and why will you assemble each of these segments of the population.

When, where and why will you asemble your segment of the population.

Service to various publics depends to a considerable degree upon
the effective involvement of many volunteers in the work of community
development. Many citizens, in addition to professional staff, will have
to understand the factors involved. Some leaders, at least, will have
to identify possible solutions as well as develop a plan of action which
in itself will require an educational process for the public concerned.
The following questions parallel the steps which must be followed in organizing any program:

What are the first steps which have to be taken in identifying
and recruiting an audience for the contemplated program?

Do you know of any groups that are already organized who
might be interested? Who are they?

If you do not know of already organized groups, where
would you start to recruit members for a group?

In trying to set up a program, either through an already
existing group or through contacts with individuals, what
would you emphasize primarily in terms of stimulating
interest in the program?

What do you think about the various general methods which
have been suggested for recruiting participants, e. g. , lay
control, the coffee house facility, the street librarian?

Where do you think you will plan to hold your program:
organizational or agency facilities, or elsewhere? Why?

What help or assistance will you need in getting your program organized and under way? (materials, consultant,
brochures, lists.)

Participation in the development of communicative experiences
creates an opportunity for librarians to reach far out into their communities. While calling attention to significant materials, problems, and
ideas, librarians engaged in planning may help to discover and train
leaders as well as improve the overall quality of a wide variety of educational activities including conferences, institutes, workshops, and
general meetings. Program planning services directly extend a concept
of service which underlies advisory work done for individuals. A shift
in the professional point of view new defines readers' advisory service

as an area of responsibility appropriate for most librarians in their fields of subject competence. Program planners directly negotiate the index space of an entire community for help in locating appropriate materials; preparing exhibits and displays; finding suitable film materials; securing speakers; choosing appropriate topics for discussion; helping program chairmen to become more familiar with work being done by other groups and agencies.

Program planning for various consumer publics is based on the concerns and interests which have been interpreted from the data identified and organized in a continuing community study. The community development enterprise grows out of the fact that much education is constantly going on in an informal way. Community development enhances and strengthens the behavioral learning which citizens gain from their own experiences, from each other and through discussion, problem solving activities and observation. Resource specialists in media, library, and information science have finally begun to realize the approach identified by Lindeman (83) so long ago:

> The approach to adult education will be via the route of
> situations not subjects. Our academic system has grown
> in reverse order; subjects and teachers constitute the
> starting point, students are secondary. In conventional
> education the student is required to adjust himself to an
> established curriculum which is built around the student's
> needs and interests. Every adult person finds himself in
> specific situations with respect to his work, his recreation,
> his family life, his community life — situations which call
> for adjustment. Adult education begins at this point. Sub-
> ject matter is brought into the situation, is put to work when
> needed.

Additional structured learning experiences may be sought to the extent that these bear upon actual needs and interests which are awakened by some experience or by some individual. The organizing of communications experiences helps to overcome the shortcomings of trial and error learning. To the extent that a learning experience helps adults go from a need to a solution, it becomes satisfying. A citizen's educational "curriculum" includes all the activities, experiences, materials, and exchange of ideas which are employed in a cooperatively planned program. The following principles may prove useful in developing programs for service publics:

Members of the group should participate in planning and
developing work communications activities by means of
open discussion of any plans submitted by the resource
specialists.

The total program series should be divided into units, and
subunits, so that the completion of each topic can provide a
satisfactory feeling of achievement. The result is an increased interest in proceding to another unit and eventually
leads to the larger objective which was previously identified
for the program service to the user public.

In order that technical experience and specialized information
may be used in solving group problems, the leader and participants have a responsibility to supplement "common experience"
with that of experts and specialists.

While some leaders may tentatively do long-range planning
for the group, the immediate planning will shift with the progressive, cooperative evolution of member needs and interests.

If the leader is an expert in identifying participant interests,
activities and experiences he may be able to win the confidence
of the group. In such rare instances, the leader may devise
and carry out an integrated course of a formal nature which
meets the needs of the group.

Evaluation should be built into any program series and pro-
vision made for the continuous measurement of progress
in terms of goals determined or agreed upon by the group.

When organizing programs in the community, consideration
would be given to differentiation and flexibility in the offerings
made so that the needs of widely differing individuals, groups
and organizations may be served.

Program development presupposes an audience which can be assembled
in one place at one time. This does not entirely rule out a one-person
audience, but such a situation does not occur as frequently nor serve
the primary purpose of service to various publics. Group methods are
mandatory, and add a dimension to public service that may be a worthwhile counterbalance to the over-individualization of reading. Even

though no exact formula exists for program development, there appear
to be two major ways of introducing a program—either with an idea or
with an authority.

STARTING WITH AN IDEA

When starting with an idea, the issue to be started with should be
analyzed into its constituent topics. In such instances, the librarian
puts to work his understanding of selection principles by identifying the
main topic, the secondary and related topics. Some consideration should
be given as to the application to which the idea may be put, that is, what
purposes is the program designed to achieve and with whom? The consumer should be carefully delineated, indicating how the idea will appeal, and in what degree, to the audience selected.

The idea should be an "original" one to start with, for unless the
issue is important, it is difficult to create a situation where the skills
of creative and critical thinking can be employed. Issues surrounding
the idea should be identified, pro and con, with which participants and
the audience can agree or not. If this is not the case, it is difficult to
give substance to any listening, viewing or reading experiences. Certainly, if, in addition, the idea can be visualized, greater impact and
depth of meaning is likely to occur.

The subject, or main idea, should be timely and related to community
trends or its timeliness be made evident by relating it to other items
in the news. If the subject is sufficiently interesting and its presentation
timely, any audience can be expected to have questions. As many questions as possible should be anticipated, perhaps under some such structure
as the following: (1) points requiring fuller treatment, (2) points of
disagreement, (3) points not covered.

As is typical in any resource agency sponsored program, further
learning is encouraged in order to deepen and to prolong the attention-
getting initial interest. Take-homes are usually available, such as
specially prepared reading lists or, circulated services can be made
available for materials or related interest displayed on the spot. Other
resource services such as reference and readers' advisory may be
brought to the attention of the audience. Programs sponsored by other
agencies in the community may be referred to and, thus, a major responsibility is discharged by the agency's clearing house function.

STARTING WITH AN AUTHORITY

The usual alternative to starting with an idea is to begin the program with an authority who has been carefully selected from the community resource file, as one who is so familiar with his subject, that he talks quite freely about it. In most instances, such a resource person will possess or have access to materials that will enrich his presentation. These resources may be visuals, or valuable suggestions, as to other specialists who could be interviewed about the topic of concern. An informal and relaxed person is usually personable and interesting but these assets, in themselves, are not enough to carry a program to successful completion.

In recruiting an authority around whom one expects to build a program, some cautions are in order. The person should not be selected simply out of a feeling of obligation because of many hours devoted to committee work either for the library or for any other agency. Neither should the authority be one who has few assets other than the fact of his status as the head of a department or even an agency, and this does not exclude library department heads. Because of the press of duties and other imperatives, such persons often do not have the time to be spontaneous and may have to use excessive notes or resort to memorization. Such limitations will have a detrimental effect upon the quality of the subsequent program in which they participate.

Fitting technique to purpose is required because some plan and order is necessary in group activity in order to ensure purposeful communication. If meaning is allowed to occur haphazardly, it may at a later date have to be corrected. Efficiency in communication is accomplished by fitting appropriate technique to the specific purposes sought. Purposes can range over those which reach for information, for understanding, for problem-solving, or skill development.

If information is sought in the communications situation, then one could consider as a technique a speaker who is informed and whose message is organized. As an alternative, one of the audiovisuals might be satisfactory—particularly a film, a videotape, or a slide presentation that can carry an integrated message. For a smaller group, the working paper can serve as a satisfactory substitute. When the panel used is of a symposium format, information can be communicated directly and be fairly effective.

If understanding is the purpose of the structured communication, then something more than the speaker, the film or the working paper is needed. These information techniques may be used as a brief introduction, but they should be supplemented by the panel discussion, role play, and straight discussion. In these techniques, understanding is better achieved because information is shared and considered from different points of view.

If problem-solving is the goal of the communications situation, then any of the techniques for information and understanding may be used to define the problem. Once defined and analyzed, it is commonly expected that some action will develop. In order to promote action, a solution must be worked out through the technique of a meeting structure. Consensus should be reached at each step of the agenda or else no final agreement is ever likely to occur.

If the development of a skill is the objective of the communication or the learning enterprise, then any technique considered above can be used as long as it leads to involvement. When a skill is developed, habit patterns are usually changed or new ones formed. Consequently, involvement in the skill-producing activity is of primary importance, and is induced most directly through techniques such as the case study, and extended practice periods.

PREPARING THE MATERIALS

Starting with an idea, or speaker, does not mean stopping there, particularly on television. One should not underestimate the need for showing as well as speaking. What is seen is as important as what is heard. Every visual must have a purpose, as indeed must every word, and be simplified to the barest essentials. It must be remembered that in the initial segment of every program, brevity almost to the point of labeling is essential for instant appeal. If the viewer is going to switch channels, he will do so in the first half minute. To the extent that a program audience is articulate concerning its needs and interests, some individuals in the group should play an increasingly important role in determining the materials which will most adequately serve their needs and fulfill their interests.

Within limits of these principles, program materials should be determined cooperatively by both group members and leader. Participants should contribute according to their particular abilities, experience and special interests.

Where individual background, experience and ability
in a group make classification desirable, materials
of varying difficulty, or activities of different types
should be developed cooperatively with participants
on the basis of interests, experiences or capacity to
do the work.

Where materials and content are of a broad nature,
program series should be built around emergency
situations which can be identified in the life situations
of participants.

Table 5. Program Meeting Agenda

1. What is our purpose? .To help pre- and retired people continue living interesting and creative lives? .To develop a program for this group at low cost to the consumer	.Who needs to know what about this purpose?
2. Who is our consumer public? .What are their interests and charac-teristics? .Where are they located? Where can they be reached?	.What is the best time to reach them?

3. What topics are they interested in?
 	
.Orientation to...
   Sources of information, education & assistance.
 	
.Financial and legal aspects...
   Getting the most for your money, consumer education.
   Putting your hobby or interest to work (or former occupation).
 	
.Creative use of leisure time...
   Enriched living.
   Citizen in politics, chance to do something for democracy.
	.Resources: who can give what kind of help to best advantage?

.Your health...
  Physical care.
  Mental (health) attitudes towards living.

.Your family...
  How to live independent of other generations.

.Living arrangements & accomodation...

.Terminal session...
  Where do we go from here?

4. Techniques

.Transmit information

.Understand a problem, or variety of viewpoints

.Solve a problem

.Develop a skill

5. Administration & coordination

.Developing session content...

.When and where to begin, suitable locations, meeting time and frequency...

.Publicity, registration...

Processes

.Direct personal mailing lists of aging persons

.Radio and television

.Newspapers and newsletters

.Mailing to organizations and agencies business, industry, unions, personnel managers, etc.

SEVEN

PLANNING AND EVALUATION

Planning and evaluation go hand in hand and are probably the most important aspects in program development. Planning and evaluation are complicated matters and often become complex primarily because changes in people's behavior are involved. As a result of theory and experimentation, there are a number of principles involved which can serve as useful guidelines for the librarian in program development. These are important for the librarian to consider since evaluation of behavior has for so many years been a forbidden area of concern in the profession.

Seldom included among these principles and often overlooked by the program planner is the direct and symbiotic relation between planning and evaluation. The end product can no more be left to chance in program development than it can in an industrial process. The outcomes or consequences must be specified as well as the means to be employed to collect data about them. The outcomes are changes in behavior which the participants do not have at the beginning of a program but which they can be expected to have at the end of it as a result of involvement in the program sequence. This implies that behavioral objectives should be specified in addition to the non-behavioral purposes which are usually given.

Each social agency has its particular set of guidelines for developing program demonstrations or research projects. In general, all of these guidelines follow the general problem solving model. There is an initial identification of the problem together with a statement describing previous solutions and an analysis of why they have failed. This analysis leads into the demonstration being proposed and why it will succeed where others have failed. The proposed program is described. Then an indication of the benefits to be realized will preface a section on the purpose of evaluation and the methods to be employed.

Communication is a process of change. Everyone who communicates does so because he wants to affect human behavior. When a resource professional goes into service in a particular community, success will depend to a great extent upon how well he can analyze and interpret three major factors: the situation, the people involved, and himself in relation to the situation and the people involved. Change agents who want to introduce new ideas must accurately observe the situation and the audiences with which they must deal.

The Situation: No matter how familiar the professional change agent may be with other communities and their library services, he will find it profitable to examine the new situation in some detail. Previous experience and knowledge will suggest some things to look for, and the professional may be able to interpret or explain some events in new ways. It is more important to study and determine why local conditions are as they are. The professional should seek an understanding of causes and not be content with surface explanations and excuses. It is not his function to criticize, but rather to use the collected and interpreted information creatively in furthering community objectives. It is easy, for example, to accept such explanations as "insufficient funds" or "untrained personnel."

It is more difficult, but more rewarding, to analyze the current utilization of resources and determine whether other courses of action are available. In this regard, it is of fundamental importance to find out how decisions are made in the community, who makes them, and especially what bases are used for decision making. What is the formal structure of the community? Is it shaped like a triangle, with a power structure at the top and a descending order of power as the structure grows broader toward the base? Are subdivisions of power rigidly observed, so that the citizen can only talk to persons who sit at the various agencies' public desks? What kind of answers do they get? Perhaps on the other hand, the community can be thought of as a square or rectangle, with a diffused power structure and an administration at the top which assumes only nominal control?

Observe the nature, direction, and extent of change that may be taking place in the community. How was this change initiated, by whom, and over what problems? Is there a fixed or flexible priority for the utilization of personnel and materials when the needs arise in the community? Perhaps the cause for current developments may have been a change in some agency personnel. Perhaps a highly competent person has been removed and his job filled by someone less capable, or the situation may have occured in reverse. In the presence of this change, what problems and opportunities have arisen which may need to be taken into account in adjusting citizen expectations?

Examine possible effects of new ideas which may not at first have been considered. What are the possible economic, social, political, or cultural consequences of the changes proposed. An inventory of the persons and groups likely to be affected by any new plans will enable the professional change agent to determine in advance how to take advantage of the support available, to alter plans to avoid some problems, and to deal with objectives based on problems which cannot be avoided.

The Audience: Within the systems in which the librarian operates, there are specific groups with whom he must work if new ideas are to be successful. The audience will probably be composed of relatively small face-to-face groups. Whether the audience is a dozen or millions, the number of people in that audience is not necessarily related to the essential nature of the task which is the fact that people tend to develop habits, and will resist attempts at breaking established patterns of response too quickly. They tend to reject rapid change and place high value on the knowledge, skills, and beliefs which they have already acquired.

Even the change agent's own colleagues will accept ideas only if he presents them in ways consistent with their own values. Perhaps new values of a socially higher order can be substituted and thus be made acceptable to themselves, the resource agency, and the community. Whatever the plan developed it will involve new ways of behaving for the audience. Listeners will make changes suggested to them only as they are ready and able to make them. By careful observation their readiness to change can be determined as well as the success of what has already been attempted. It may be necessary to break major new ideas into many small ideas and to observe carefully what happens before, during and after each one is introduced in order to determine how to proceed. Plans and goals may have to be modified many times.

Yourself: No inventory of factors of success is at all complete unless the agent of change describes himself. Self-appraisal may be much more difficult but the ability to understand and correct deficiencies greatly increases the chance of success. The following questions may serve as a useful guide to self-evaluation:

Do you fully understand the assumptions that you made perhaps unconsciously about community characteristics, needs, and problems?

Have you acquired the knowledge and ability to accomplish
the changes necessary in this community? Or, will a lack
of technique betray you once the program is underway?

Can you place yourself in the role of listener and observer?
Do you criticize those who disagree with you rather than try
to understand and reconcile their view with yours?

Do you have an honest picture of how you get along with
your associates? Are you prepared to remedy those personal factors which seem to interfere with good relationships between you and those around you?

Communication design is the decision of what to do within certain
constraints. A constraint is something which forces, compels, or ob-
liges, or which confines forcibly. Actually the constraints on communication design, like social or economic constraints, are considered
more positively as guides and opportunities in the total environment
within which the professional resource person works. Constraints are
accepted by the professionally mature change agent as rules of the game
to be used to advantage, and partly as challenges to be overcome with
ingenuity and creativeness.

Constraints which are more difficult to overcome are called limiting
factors. Those limiting factors which can still be overcome and turned
into breakthroughs for better design are called strategic factors. The
constraints in total are called critical factors which are important elements of any communications program. Critical factors may be turned
into strategic factors by good systems design, or, as a result of a lack
of experience, they may remain limiting factors and prevent carrying
out the program at all.

In systems design, the constraints must be listed, and the limiting
factors isolated for analysis, in order to list those factors which can
be moved to strategic factors. This is an essential part of the problem
solving process. The problem solver starts out with an almost unlimited
number of possibilities before recycling possible solutions in the light
of experience in the program. In the meantime, aggressive action pur-
sues the necessary information instead of waiting for it to happen along
by itself. Media, library, and information specialists aim at developing
new programs, resources and services for the purpose of using them to
meet social needs.

PLANNING TO MEET OBJECTIVES

Resource specialists in media, library and information science have always held their agency purposes in fairly sharp focus and, depending upon resources, have established programs in conformity with goals. Unfortunately, the goals have not always been realistically formulated or aimed towards the constituency for whom they have been designed. Like any other social professional, resource change agents have been challenged by a new set of imperatives which require an enhanced awareness of the interdependence of communication media in maximizing learning.

The research done in learning and communications theory supports the principles of reinforcement in the community situation, and suggests a more perceptual approach to an understanding of communication than either linear logic or the stimulus response approach to meaning is able to supply. Be this as it may, certain factors become fundamental elements in the process of program planning to meet the newer social imperatives.

Analyze your social agency in order to understand why it is interested in certain publics. Consideration of resources and services offered by the resource center are important, but also of particular significance are those available from other social, educational and communications agencies. No single agency in the community is in as favorable a position as the media, library and information center to discharge the responsibilities of a coordinating structure.

An agency self study is also, to an extent, an analysis of the resource center's image. For example, the book may predominate in this library in all its stuffy spendor, or the librarians in that library may be oriented towards a more open-ended learning experience for all people. In the latter instance, media will predominate, including a wide range of materials and equipment in order to reduce the level of abstraction in the subject collections.

Analyze your publics, in the plural, because the community (whether public, academic, or special) is not one amorphous mass. It is composed of individuals who have many characteristics in common with many others. These common characteristics become the "subject headings," under which resource specialists analyze their publics and group them into categories so as to beam messages to them with specialized content that can be expected to catch and hold their awareness. It is by

means of such methods that retrieval systems are built and user studies
are of particular significance in helping to answer such questions as:
(1) Whom do you wish to reach? (2) Where can you reach them? (3)
When can you reach them?

Users of community resources are in a sense committed to, or at
least, partially involved in, media, library, and information services.
But since users represent such a small element in the total population,
potential publics must be analyzed as well. As a result of a community
study, interests and concerns will be identified, and emerge as characteristics under which people can be grouped, and programs developed in
order to catch and hold their attention. Such utilization of motivational
planning is necessary because meaning emerges only when information
becomes kinetic, i. e., related to real-life interests.

Analyze your resources in order to determine whether the resources
and the materials available are pertinent to the interests and abilities
of the publics to be reached. In addition, it is important to have resources in sufficient duplication. When a specific title, for example,
is mentioned on a mass media program, are there enough copies to
cope with the demand for it? Resource surveillance keeps one aware
of public media programming and the demands that are likely to occur.

Beyond the agency infrastructure, many other resources exist in
the community which could be utilized were they identified and organized for use. Audiovisual and printed materials, as well as persons
with special capabilities are available and could be given wider ex-
posure. When resource persons are identified, they can be made a-
vailable to others through one of the center's reference tools known as
a community resource file. Another reference tool, the community
calendar, identifies the program and other organized activities of
groups, and lists them for wide perusal.

Campaign planning is a method used by change agents to focus attention upon an objective and a particular public to be reached. To
program without reference to a target group, is to disperse one's efforts and to scatter one's effectiveness in a wasteful misuse of resource
potential. The "Friends" organization is an example of a satellite
group, which can render invaluable assistance both in specific group
programming, and in making it difficult for people to avoid thinking
about the particular issue at hand.

When media are orchestrated around an issue, it becomes easier
to precipitate an ever widening involvement of people in the community

studying the need for change. For example, in any library campaign
for community education about an issue, there are at least three levels
of program development. At first, it is necessary to introduce the topic
and the social group relationship to it based on some plan of action:

What to say? What ideas can be presented in order to involve
new patrons and hold those already involved?

Where to say it? What media to employ and within which
channel will maximum involvement occur?

How to say it and present persuasive arguments in the most
interesting and convincing manner (e. g. , the sociodrama
model of hero and villian) ?

How much programming? At what point does the law of
diminishing returns operate?

How can promotion and campaign planning be related to
results with what effect in some evaluative design?

At the next level of development, selective dissemination of information helps to open up the topic for various publics. Mailing lists are
organized, for example, around the characteristics of the audiences to
be reached. Speakers and films can be selected to accomplish, by means
of programs for the smaller group, what readers' advisory and reference
services can do for the individual.

Finally, on the widest level of all, the mass media can create an
awareness in the public at large of the issue of concern to the community,
i. e. , concern about a particular issue can be simultaneously introduced
on television, radio and newspapers and pursued by means of them in
a number of variations in an effort to reach groups whenever convenient
for them, and wherever they may happen to be. Commentary on the issues which have been introduced, and greater depth of presentation can
be effected through magazines, newspaper articles, and program planning.

EVALUATION OF OUTCOMES

Evaluation offers the greatest potential benefit if it is a longtime,
continuous, and built-in part of the total communications process. One-
shot evaluations are insufficient. The evaluation of communicative activity is better when concerned with outcomes, with results, with changes

in people. If results of evaluation are fed back to help in the redefinition of goals and improvement of approach, the whole communicative effort can benefit. Evaluation should be more concerned with results than with energy spent. Numbers of films shown, books borrowed, program hours scheduled, money spent, broadcasts made, and conferences attended may account for time and energy but in themselves reveal little evidence of changes brought about in behavior.

Self-appraisal usually is better than appraisal by outsiders if it is done in an honest and self-reflecting manner. Evaluation surveys by "outside experts" which do not adequately involve local people frequently result in little improvement. As a process, evaluation has most value to those who go through it. The professional change agent who becomes most deeply involved in evaluation will grow most. Everyone concerned with the communicative effort should be involved in evaluation. It can be at any level. The board evaluates; an administrator or supervisory team can evaluate; and the staff can be brought into the process. More beneficial, however, is the involvement of patrons, club members and everyone else taking part. The public, too, evaluates, sometimes directly and other times through elected representatives.

Evaluation is always made in terms of objectives or goals. There are essentially two major types of evaluation: congruency and contingency. Congruency evaluation uses an absolute set of standards against which a program is measured. The weakness of this type of evaluation is that the standards are frequently set in a sterile context and may not apply to the situation being evaluated. A contingency evaluation utilizes the consequences of the process as it occurs and attempts to determine if it has met the goals and objectives. Its weakness lies in the fact that a lot of rationalization tends to creep into the evaluative process.

In communication, the outcome desired is a change in behavior. Both the participants and the leader (agency) have objectives for communicative activity, and must be in fundamental agreement in order for a successful program to emerge. If progress is being made, repeated evaluation will show the stages of growth toward accepted objectives. Long-term objectives are usually ideals. To induce some feeling of success among participants, short-term program goals must be set for them.

In the past, personal objectives of individuals have determined to a large extent the programming in certain agencies. But public agencies should also be concerned with objectives which are consistent with the

objectives of the supporting social order. In a democracy, the highest
human power which sets learning objectives for an adult is the adult
himself as well as the majority will of his peers. The professional
task is to identify and define educational needs and interests in harmony
with the objectives of participants. Setting adequate objectives is the
major concern of evaluation and is a valuable outcome. Objectives to
be worthwhile must be: (1) expressed in terms of behavior, (2) clearly
and specifically stated, (3) widely understood and accepted by all involved in a learning activity (4) attainable, (5) recognized as potentially
changing.

     Whether objectives arise from organic (biological), or environmental
(social, cultural, spiritual) forces, they constitute the "developmental
tasks" of participants at successive ages in their particular life span.
Some evidence of behavior change is more valid than others. Some evidence comes closer than others to indicating true behavior. Evaluation
in communication is usually a compromise between collecting imperfect-
but-easy-to-obtain evidence and what is considered to be valid evidence
of growth and change. A single index, while desired by the layman,
seldom satisfies the professional person. Perhaps the following outline
may prove useful in planning and evaluation.

Planning Principles

          An effective program must be adapted to the kind of
          community which the agency serves and be related
          to the people's needs.

          The agency must be aware of the vital issues which
          concern the community, and aware of what it (the
          agency) can do to increase understanding of these
          vital issues.

          A good program depends on an intelligent materials
          development policy — one that is related to the com-
          munity's needs and interests.

          A good program depends on a basic understanding of
          the assumptions underlying the need and development
          of such a program.

          A good program depends on staff participation and
          training.

Participation by local groups in the planning and design
process is essential.

Planning Steps

Community interest, needs and available resources
determine where a promising start may be made.
Those who are definitely interested may constitute
the group of initial recruits.

A start with less difficult community problems or
activities helps volunteers branch out into more comprehensive and complex undertakings. It is important to get extensive participation in thought, discussion,
and planning.

Recruits to the work group must understand their
particular contribution to the program and how it
fits into the total series. Volunteers must acquire
a feeling of success in readily achieving success in
some preliminary activities.

Emphasis should be placed on the development of each
group member. Rotation of leadership is advisable so
that no centralization of control develops. Consequently,
continuous training in leadership and participant roles
is a valuable product of such involvement.

Community endorsement is important, not only by community leaders, but by other groups and agencies. Coordination of plans with efforts being made by others interested in a similar purpose is desirable.

Group members should be aware of tensions, problems,
needs and aspirations of the community and work to integrate their efforts and successes into the larger aspects of community development. Action groups motivate
learning through involvement in projects that are obviously needed by other people.

Evaluation Principles

Services and programs should arise from expressions of individual and group interests. Materials, experiences and

activities have to be drawn from and produced around the actual
life interests and problems of participants.

Do programs and services permit cooperative
participation by every volunteer and serve the
purposes determined by the group?

Are the materials and experiences within the
understanding of participants and adapted to individual differences with the group?

Services and programs should provide manual, intellectual,
and emotional activity; free, informal discussion; as well as
association and cooperative endeavor in order to satisfy a
feeling of progress and achievement by participants.

What opportunity is there for volunteers to
choose, plan and evaluate the communicative
procedures in the series?

Are various types of sensory experience (visual,
audio, movement) required as well as the appre-
ciative, creative and reflective activities?

Services and programs have to contain accurate information
as well as dependable suggestions and directions for securing
materials and information, both from group experiences and
other sources such as printed, audio-visual, and community
resources.

Services and programs should provide stimulus to further
learning and carry over (transfer) from group activities
to pertinent situations in home, neighborhood, and community as well as solve other related problems arising
from life situations.

Are subunits integrated in the whole and comprehensive enough to ensure a gradual achievement
of satisfaction?

Can the present scope of participant interest be
enlarged and enriched in opportunities to carry
interest throughout the programs and into other
related series?

Evaluative Steps

Continuing evaluation of purposes, planning, and procedures should be conducted. Evaluation results should be considered thoughtfully by all persons involved in the action group. Interpretation may be based on the following criteria and procedures:

Criteria which state the assumptions relating to:

Creation of a plan.

Utilization of resources.

Procedures utilized.

Points for evaluation.

Criteria which interpret the fulfillment of objectives for:

Individual participant outcomes.

Agency organization and development.

Program design and communication.

Community development and coordination.

Criteria which interpret the operational effeciency of:

Organizational procedures and administration.

Citizen committee coordination.

Various agency staff coordination.

Resource and physical facility deployment.

Communicative procedures and leadership.

Wide variety of procedures are available for data
collection:

Statistical compilations of behavior
patterns.

Direct and self-observational samples.

Narrative accounts of behavior development.

Performance under simulated conditions.

Survey of sample or complete conditions.

Determine "back-home" applications.

Appraisal judgments by expert panel.

AGENCY-COMMUNITY RELATIONS AS CRITERIA MATRIX

Separate media, library, and information agencies are often considered to be but prototypes of an integrated communications resource
center for the community. Some of these agencies have already begun
to identify community needs and interests as well as serve as coordinating structures without which efforts towards community integration
are severely handicapped. In any community there are various agencies
and institutions organized in order to achieve some social purpose, or
to give expression to the varying interests of like-minded people. Because of their importance some of these agencies have been given legal
status and sanction. The resource center is one of these, delegated as
it is by the community to perform continuing services of an informational
and educational nature.

Each agency which enters some aspect of the field of community endeavor, usually in response to public pressure, has tended to operate
its own service program without reference to the activities of others.
Without wide sensitivity for the varying interests and needs of the public,
the librarian remains a custodian of the book and a staunch supporter
of the traditional type of library as a necessary element in a specialized
society. But Mial makes the point that it is, "undesirable and unhealthy
to rationalize as specialization what the psychiatrist calls 'ritual avoid-
ance' of areas that threaten our security (92)." More recently, Blakeley (1

has indicated that two diametrically opposed philosophies still tragically compete for the librarian's attention in the "four walls" philosophy of community endeavor:

> Our choice is between continuing to try to flee
> individually from our common problems and
> turning to face them together; between contin-
> uing to behave like passive victims of social
> forces and trying to act like positive agents in
> their control; between continuing to live in ac-
> cord with the 'four walls' philosophy, or be-
> ginning to live in accord with the philosophy of
> community renewal.

Two basic approaches have been used to provide coordination and direction of community services for adults. Community organization and community development are the methods which describe a relation-ship for communication and learning which the resource agency can de-cide to establish and use. Any difference between community organ-ization and community development is a matter of degree. Both dis-count the unilateral approaches of public relations and the type of media service which considers organization in terms of a single agency and which in the past has been such a ubiquitous and discouraging character-istic of community endeavor. Community organization and community development are not mutually exclusive endeavors and their aim is not to destroy existing community structure but to make it possible for an increasing number of people to participate in community decision-making processes.

Community involvement can provide a realistic matrix for leader-ship training and for the practice of various types of interactive exper-iences. Vivid living data is readily available about human group be-havior and enables the participant in leadership training to become a more effective observer and participant. Back in agency meetings, diagnostic sessions can analyze such experiences and provide the frame-work for interpretation and understanding. Materials can be system-atically examined and other resources brought to bear in order to under-stand and to generalize about communications endeavor in the community. Assumptions about social organization and human values can be tested so as to improve the individual's ability to help in social situations with-out over-reliance upon rigid techniques of conducting meetings or man-ipulating people.

The community organization method emphasizes the administration and the coordination of resources as a basic prerequisite for the eventual development of educational and informational programs. Service to citizens is too large for any one agency to provide and requires the combined planning of all organizations and the coordinating service of some one group which continually investigates, plans, and acts in the interest of the community as a whole. Media, library, and information service is uniquely constituted to perform this function of coordination.

The realization of a concept of a coordinating structure is at the heart of communication systems development. As media, library, and information specialists cooperate more meaningfully among themselves they will be in a better position to exert coordinative leadership in community development. The responsibilities of a coordinating structure (33) are as follows:

Promote continuous study and review of the community.

Identify the information and educational needs and interests of various publics in the community.

Identify community resources that can be used for programming as well as the various programs sponsored by agencies and groups in the community.

Provide a clearinghouse and publicize information about needs, interests, resources, and programs.

Develop informational and educational programs, or see that they are developed by others in order to make it difficult for people to avoid thinking about major problems of community life.

Promote evaluation and research in terms of community goals and objectives.

The accomplishment of policies as significant as these to the whole community, educationally, and informationally, should not be left to chance or to the individual and uncoordinated efforts of various agencies and groups. Are any of the responsibilities of a coordinating structure beyond the function of resource center service? When one examines the record of public statements by leaders in the profession and the various statements of standards, it becomes increasingly difficult to point to any single responsibility listed above for a coordinating structure that is not an integral element of media, library, and information service. This is especially true for any publicly supported agency.

For example, the process of coordination is initiated by resource center interests with the appointment of a citizens' study committee for the community development education. Initially a single group, the committee gradually proliferates itself as it subdivides for more special- ized purposes, or as the need and desire for participation is generated in the neighborhoods and through the activities of motivated organizations and groups. Many people can be readily involved in the evaluation of agency programs and an increased concern over study and research will appear as the effort is made to base effective recommendations upon valid and appropriate data. As this motivation to participate in- creases in scope and depth and as it is demonstrated in activities sup- porting broad community development efforts, learning will take place.

Community development, to be effective, requires the extensive in- volvement of volunteers as a continuing educational experience for them. Criticism of the use of volunteers has been, of course, a long-standing concern in media, library, and information service. This criticism is probably justified given the types of activities to which volunteers were at one time assigned. Volunteers were asked to assume the tasks of clericals and non-professionals because the budget was not large enough to employ this type of staff member. In other words, volunteers were used to get a job done for nothing. Obviously the rate of turnover of such "staff members" was phenomenal and tended to demoralize even further the already grossly underpaid employees. The profession has scarcely yet overcome such unfortunate experiences.

The intelligent use of volunteers, however, is a basic element in the program of any agency seeking effective liaison with, and involvement in the community to any extent. In general, volunteers need orientation and some training in those types of activities in which they can readily perceive an immediate relevance to their own life situation, e.g., training in story telling, leadership training, program-planning clinics, speaking assignments, public relations programs, community study projects, agency development, and extension services. All of these projects can be liberally staffed with volunteers to their own advantage and to that of the agency's program in the community. The fact of their involvement is usually the beginning of an educational and developmental experience for themselves, not only in one specific activity but also its relation to total resource services in the community.

The resources of the community media, library and information
agency are supplemented by a plethora of other information centers and
services, especially in metropolis. These agencies serve limited
clienteles and usually with specialized collections and services. Few
if any specialized agencies are directly responsible to the community
and even where the public may have some claim on their services, their
administration is removed by several steps from actual commitment
to individuals, organizations, and groups in the community. This is
not to say that many specialized libraries have not worked for the betterment of the whole community or have not placed their resources and
services behind the leadership of public librarians, but it soon becomes
evident to the community activist that only the administration of the
public library, if any, can see the community whole and meet a direct
responsibility to all publics and interests.

The public librarian has the broadest mandate or commission to
administer public educational and informational services in any community (13). The community librarian is responsible to the entire community and has direct access to all the people and their representatives
in contrast to all other types of librarians who, at best, work with the
executive officer of their institution. Traditionally, there has been no
group, interest, or individual to whom the public librarian may deny
information and educational services. The open door is traditional but
has remained largely a passive accommodation to those who seek it out.
Only in a very few instances have particular community librarians responded to the opportunities of this social mandate.

The library trustee has an active role to fill in helping the librarian
relate to and fulfill his obligations in the community. For example, it
is the library board which must establish a policy of making buildings
and grounds attractive and then to apply the policy through responsible
committees (59). Library trustees can help the staff in motivating new-
comers and others to participate in library services and in recruiting
a wide range of volunteers for activities associated with community
programming. The trustee can be indispensable in maintaining a climate
for the free exchange of ideas and for thorough discussions of community problems and proposed solutions. The trustees have a serious and
important role to fill in keeping the channels of communication and information open to all citizens. They also must see that the administrative control documents of purposes and policies are freely available
to all groups and segments of the community as a basis for understanding
library needs. Finally, the trustees have a role to play in promoting
cooperative arrangements among librarians of all types in order to bring
improved communication services to all residents (35).

There are probably any number of reasons why cooperative activity among resource specialists of various types and between librarians and community agencies has been retarded. But a few of them can be mentioned as challenges and goals for an integrated profession to consider. The administrative infrastructure under which most libraries operate is a serious obstacle making all but unilateral operations nearly impossible. The lack of communication among resource specialists of various sorts makes it difficult for them, and certainly impossible for their publics, to understand the various communication functions, policies and programs. That types of agencies overlap, as in school and public libraries, where the distinction in service to children and youth is extremely tenuous and hardly defensible, is a serious handicap in the competition for financial support. Situations such as the problem of service to youth have been allowed to develop until solutions become increasingly difficult.

Another serious problem which may underlie those already mentioned is the absence of almost any planning, especially of a long-range nature, that would take advantage of the various media and other electronic developments on the horizon. Stone (134) has made it obvious that the library function needs to be redefined. Technological developments already exist, even without the videophone and cablevision, to bring resource service to people where they are and not where the center happens to be located. All that is lacking is the will to use available resources. Certainly capital investment in the new technology would not seem so far beyond the realm of possibility if resource specialists were to reexamine expensive present services such as the branch library system which, with the videophone and cablevision, has become obsolete.

A staff which conducts continuing study of the community is more likely to be aware of trends and shifts in the local scene which could represent a problem in the making. Such a library will have on hand resources, reports and studies needed for community-wide planning. Essentially the staff becomes informed as to who the people are that develop messages and programs about what topics and the time and place of such activity. Phinney makes the following point:

> "Community agencies can be helpful in assisting
> librarians to assess their services and adapt them
> to new conditions and a different and unfamiliar
> clientele. They may be able to point out areas in
> which flexibility of routines is needed, and also
> where new methods of making the resources of a
> whole area more fully accessible to the professional
> may be employed." (114)

A community is not composed of mutually exclusive groups whose characteristics can be definitely delineated. Individuals are often members of different groups, the extent of whose access to resource services varies considerably. It is often fortuitous that any one individual has access to the quality of communication services needed to live a productive and continuously developing form of life. The interests and educational needs of these individuals vary in range and intensity both in point of time and as compared with other members of their groups. To identify the elements which comprise a community, the professional requires a knowledge of its characteristics and resources, as well as an awareness of the less obvious factors affecting it.

It is often argued that there must be a considerable increase in the number and quality of resource centers. But it must be remembered that as far as the more populated areas of the nation are concerned, metropolis is glutted with resource agencies—public, school, college, university, special. The lack seems to be, rather, in statesmanship, together with a pervasive unwillingness to consider the problems from a coordinative point of view. Cooperation implies the use of energy and vigorous activity directed towards accomplishing the task of coordination among libraries and other resource units in the community. Even where librarians of various sorts do cooperate with one another, albeit in a limited sort of way, there is frequently a failure to draw on the community, or special groups, or those who represent the power structure (46).

It has sometimes been said that the area of greatest duplicity in library science is the discrepancy between the concept of cooperation and the actual implementation of cooperative activity. Many articles appear regularly in all types of journals (23) and cooperation is exhorted as a foundation stone for excellence, and as a way of achieving strength and of providing unlimited access to information. In practice however, the realities outweight good intentions. These realities include such factors as immediate personal gain from the venture, unwillingness to relinquish a measure of complete antonomy or to share in the group benefits of the venture.

Cooperation alone, with all due respect to the outstanding examples, does not seem to attack the basic problems. Such planning has worked towards greater utilization of conventional solutions like larger collections and cooperative processing of book materials. But imaginative planning is needed immediately to meet such rapidly changing conditions as explosive information requirements, revolutionary technological advances and the swiftly changing nature of people's needs. Planning to meet such needs cannot occur effectively until the administrative and legal restrictions are abolished which have hampered adequate coordination.

Possibly the single most critical factor in the ineffectiveness of cooperation has been the attitude of librarians towards community development. Little effort is made to make communication services known, let along attempt to use such "Madison Avenue" devices as marketing research and product experimentation. Hopefully, the interaction of some professional leaders with community groups and interests will continue to increase and force a reorientation of librarianship towards community development education. Then the community will be seen as a major source of program content and a guide to integration in the collaborative study of common areas of concern.

The community can be readily programmed with situations in which people can develop their sensitivity and their courage, and obtain social nourishment and perspective. Community organization and community development are the major social methods used by people to realize their interests and needs. Organizations are the media through which people try to reach their goals whether these goals call for evolutionary change or revolutionary activism.

EVALUATIVE CRITERIA

At this point it may be desirable to provide an example of how the preceeding criteria can be applied to a specific program or service in a community. First, a few assumptions must be made to provide a background for a community program to evaluate. Assume that a change agent has been active in the formation of a drug rehabilitation program in an urban community. Also assume that this program began as a result of an expressed need by a group of individuals in the community representing the medical profession, educators, lay citizens, politicians, law enforcement officials, and religious leaders.

A drug rehabilitation center has been established through a federal grant. The continuation of the program is dependent upon this federal grant. The major objective of this program is the rehabilitation of all drug users so that they might return to productive community life. In other words, the major consequence of this program is to rehabilitate drug users. A second consequence is to discourage others from becoming drug users and a third is to provide an early detection or warning system for drug users or potential drug users.

Criteria which interpret the fulfillment of objectives for the individual participants are:

Did the program provide services that fostered drug rehabilitation?

Where did the program fail to meet individual needs?

Was the program explained completely and in an understandable manner?

Was the program flexible enough to meet all needs?

Were the resources adequate and applied effectively?

Was there a follow-up after treatment was completed?

Is individual privacy respected and protected?

Criteria which interpret the fulfillment of objectives for the agency organization and development are:

Are the objectives clearly stated and understood by everyone in the agency?

Are the resources adequate to meet the agency's objectives?

Are channels of communication within the agency and with outside cooperating agencies open, available, and easy to use?

Do staff members understand their responsibilities and authority?

Are staff members competent to perform their duties to meet their responsibilities?

Is the agency susceptible to change from within and from the outside?

Is the agency client oriented?

Has the agency established measures of performance?

Does the agency keep adequate records to evaluate its performance and account for its use of resources?

Is the agency sensitive to new areas in which its resources may be applied?

Is the agency meeting its objectives?

Criteria which interpret the fulfillment of objectives for program design and communication are:

Is the program structured to meet the objectives?

Is the program making best use of its resources?

Is the program producing the desired effects in an effective and efficient manner?

Is the program locked into a single mode of operation?

Does the program meet the needs of the participants?

Can the program be changed easily?

What would be the consequences of a change in the program?

Is the program geared to handle the case load?

Are there areas the program, as designed, cannot adequately handle?

Are channels of communication designed into the program or have they simply grown?

Does the program provide for feedback?

Is the program designed around the client?

What effects does the program have on the client?

What effects does the client have on the program?

How does the program involve outside resources and cooperating agencies?

Who needs to know what about this program?

Does the community understand the objectives and operation of the program?

Criteria which interpret the fulfillment of community development and coordination are:

What effect does this program have on the community?

What effect does the community have on this program?

What controls does the community exert over the program and the agency?

Who in the community are actively involved in this program?

Do those in the community who are involved in the program represent a power group?

What use is made of volunteers?

What other community agencies are involved in the program?

What is the role of other community agencies or groups?

How does the role of other community individuals, agencies or groups promote or detract from the objectives of the program?

What is the coordinating structure of the community individuals, groups, or agencies involved?

What are some examples of how the community has developed as a result of this program?

What are some examples that demonstrate the effectiveness of coordination in this program or lack thereof?

Criteria which interpret the operational efficiency of the organizational procedures and administration are:

Do individuals have authority to match their responsibilities?

Are procedures well documented and followed?

Are decisions made in a timely judicious manner?

What are some examples of the decision making process at all levels in the organization?

Are policies open for change?

Is the organizational structure such that bidirectional
communication is possible?

Are staff members involved in decision making?

Does the organizational structure foster the meeting
of goals and objectives?

Does the organizational structure promote individual
initiative?

Are procedures simplified as much as possible?

Are adequate controls over procedures apparent?

Have situations arisen for which there are no procedures?

Are procedures and personnal evaluated periodically?

Is there a feedback mechanism to monitor procedures
and organizational structure?

What are the bottlenecks in the present procedures?

What plans have been formulated for future development?

What scheduling procedures are utilized?

Criteria which interpret the operational efficiency of citizen committee and agency staff coordination are:

Does the citizen's committee have a communications channel open to staff members?

Is the citizen's committee involved in a meaningful way in the decision making process?

Are frequent briefings held for the citizen's committee?

Is the staff accountable to the citizen's committee in any significant way?

Are significant problems brought to the citizen's committee for solution?

Is the same information that is available to staff members also available to the citizen's committee?

Are the resources within the citizen's committee utilized by the staff for meeting the objectives of the program?

Do the staff and citizen's committee work as a unit to help the agency meet its goals?

Criteria which interpret the operational efficiency of the resources and physical facilities are:

Is the agency operating at capacity?

Are all resources and facilities being utilized to meet the stated objectives?

Are resources and facilities being optimized?

How are the resources allocated in terms of organizational structure and operating procedures?

How are the physical facilities being scheduled and utilized?

How are the resources being scheduled and utilized?

What information is used to control resource and facility allocation?

What controls are used to monitor resource and facility utilization?

What security exists for resources and facilities?

What resource allocation procedures exist?

How are decisions made regarding allocation of resources?

Who controls the resources?

Who controls utilization of physical facilities?

Criteria which interpret the operational efficiency of communicative procedures and leadership are:

Is it known by all concerned what resources are available?

Is it known by all concerned how the resources are being utilized?

Are suggestions for changes allowed to flow in all directions?

Are policies and decisions known by all concerned?

Are results of evaluation known by all concerned?

Do decisions involve all concerned?

Are the communication procedures documented and known to all?

What communicative techniques are utilized?

What cliques have evolved?

Is there a recognized leader(s)?

What style of leadership is apparent?

Is there fear of disagreement with the leadership?

What is the morale level?

Does the leadership understand their responsibilities?

The questions under each criteria can only be answered by using a variety of data collection techniques as specified earlier. It is seldom the case that a single technique can be utilized for a complex evaluative procedure. A variety of procedures act as checks and balances on one another and allow for a richer interpretation of the data collected as well as more confidence in the validity and reliability of the results.

After collecting data in the drug rehabilitation program by interviewing participants, staff members, citizen's committee members, and members of cooperating agencies as well as collecting statistical and financial information, the data can be submitted to a panel of experts for their interpretation and recommendation. In a real situation, the results of this process can then be discussed with the citizen's committee, the staff, and members of cooperating agencies for their responses, interpretation and recommendation. Essentially, the results could demonstrate that the agency had lost sight of its objectives because its survival was dependent upon federal money which was allocated based on the number of individuals treated. The program had therefore adopted a single treatment that more or less guaranteed continued treatment rather than rehabilitation.

The program's main objective had become survival as a program rather than rehabilitation and drug prevention. The channels of communication within the agency and between other individuals, agencies, and groups had deteriorated badly due to conflicting goals of other agencies as well as conflicting ideas concerning the solution to the drug problem. The citizen's committee was deprived of information and involvement and therefore took a rubber stamp approach to decision making. The program design was single-track and attempted to provide a single treatment for drug users regardless of their need. Referals to other agencies, such as psychiatric counseling services were nonexistent because of the threat of losing a client. The majority of resources were being expended to expand the organization in a bureaucratic fashion as opposed to developing services to rehabilitate drug users or prevent drug use. The agency did keep good records and provided adequate controls over information, procedures, resources, and the physical facilities. The agency was operating at capacity but due to the treatment method, this was to be expected. The leadership was authoritarian in nature with a down-only communications structure. Morale was low because of the lack of effectiveness of the program and a heavy work load. A lack of being involved in policy and decision making also contributed to low morale.

Although much more could be said based on the data collected in answer to the questions above, the significant factor was the role played by the evaluation itself. By allowing a number of involved people to participate in the evaluation, the involved participants found it to be a learning process which engendered better cooperation among all those involved and allowed them to make recommendations and propose solutions to the problems that they helped interpret from the data collected. It made them feel responsible for the program and its future success as well as recognize the need for a continuing evaluation of themselves in relation to the program.

This same type of evaluation can be applied to any community program or service including those in which a media, library or information center is directly or indirectly involved. In the example above the library was a cooperating agency primarily involved in the drug prevention and the early warning system parts of the program. The library felt it should not exert any pressure on the program until it realized that it was not being utilized. The staff, consequently, began to expand their resources on programs of their own. It was through the change agent and the evaluation that they were once again brought into the program. A more aggressive attitude on the part of the library could have facilitated a true coordinating structure and a more effective program in the first place.

BIBLIOGRAPHY

1. Robert E. Agger, <u>Rulers and the Ruled</u>. New York: Wiley, 1964.

2. Saul Alinsky, <u>Reveille for Radicals</u>. New York: Random House, 1969.

3. American Library Association, <u>Public Library Service</u>. Chicago: American Library Association, 1956.

4. American Library Association, <u>Studying the Community</u>. Chicago: American Library Association, 1960.

5. John F. Anderson, "Who Speaks for the Concerns of Library Service," <u>American Libraries</u>. 1:1062-68 (December 1970).

6. Lester Asheim, "Research in Mass Communication and Adult Reading," <u>Library Trends</u>. 6:120-40 (October 1957).

7. Lester Asheim, ed., <u>Training Needs of Librarians Doing Adult Education Work.</u> Chicago: American Library Association, 1954.

8. H. Assael, "Segmenting Markets by Group Purchasing Behavior," <u>Journal of Marketing Research</u>. 7:153-8 (May 1970).

9. Bernard Berelson, <u>Human Behavior: An Inventory of Scientific Findings</u>. New York: Harcourt, 1964.

10. Sanford Berman, "Let it all Hang Out," <u>Library Journal</u>. 96:2054-58 (June 15, 1971).

11. Robert J. Blakeley, "The Wit to Win," <u>ALA Bulletin.</u> 61:152-4; 163-9 (February 1967).

12.   Eleanor F. Brown, Library Service to the Disadvantaged.
      Metuchen, N. J.: Scarecrow, 1971.

13.   Lyman Bryson, "Foreword," in Earnestine Rose The
      Public Library in American Life. New York: Columbia
      University Press, 1954.

14.   Walter Buckley, Sociology and Modern Systems Theory.
      Englewood Cliffs, N. J.: Prentice-Hall, 1967.

15.   Mary L. Bundy, "Crisis in Library Education," Library
      Journal. 96:797-880 (March 1, 1971).

16.   Mary L. Bundy, Educating the Floating Librarian.
      Mimeographed Challenge Paper Presented for the
      Congress for Change, June 20-22, 1969.

17.   E. M. Burke, "Citizen Participation Strategies,"
      American Institute of Planners Journal. 34:287-94
      (September, 1968).

18.   Kenneth Burke, Permanence and Change. Indianapolis:
      Bobbs-Merrill, 1965.

19.   Edgar S. Cahn, "The War on Poverty: A Civilian Per-
      spective," Yale Law Journal. 73:1317-1352 (1964).

20.   J. M. Capozzola, "American Ombudsman: Problems and
      Prospects," Western Political Quarterly. 21:289-301
      (June 1968).

21.   Leon Carnovsky and Lowell Martin, eds., The Library
      in the Community. Chicago: University of Chicago
      Press, 1944.

22.   Raymond L. Carpenter, Public Library Executive:
      Exploration of the Role of an Emerging Profession.
      Contract No. OEC-2-6-068336-1462. U.S. Office
      of Education (1967).

23.   David K. Carrington, "Bibliography of Library Co-
      operation," Special Libraries. July-August 1966.

24.   C. West Churchman, The Systems Approach. New York:
      Dell Publishing, 1968.

25.   Marshall B. Clinard, Slums and Community Development.
      New York: Macmillan, 1966.

26.   Robert Colby, ed., Reaching Out (Papers in Library and
      Information Science). New Haven: Southern Connecticut
      State College, 1965.

27.   Commission on Freedom of the Press, A Free and
      Responsible Press. Chicago: University of Chicago
      Press, 1947.

28.   Ralph Conant, ed., The Public Library and the City.
      Cambridge, Massachusetts: MIT Press, 1965.

29.   K. M. Coplan and E. Castagna, eds., Library Reaches
      Out. New York: Oceana, 1965.

30.   James V. Cunningham, "Community Decision Making,"
      in Patrick R. Penland, Floating Librarians in the
      Community. Bookstore, University of Pittsburgh, 1970.

31.   Robert A. Dahl, Who Governs? New Haven: Yale
      University Press, 1961.

32.   F. J. Dempsey, "Friends of the Library," in Bowker
      Annual of Library and Book Trade Information. New
      York: Bowker, 1969.

33.   Edmund de S. Brunner, An Overview of Adult Education
      Research. Chicago: Adult Education Association, 1959.

34.   James Dickoff, "Theory in a Practice Discipline,"
      Nursing Research. 17:415-435; 545-554 (1968).

35.   Irving Dilliard, "Library Trustee and the Community,"
      Illinois Librarian. 45:249-55 (May 1963).

36.   Sidney Ditzion, Arsenals of a Democratic Culture.
      Chicago: American Library Association, 1947.

37. Hugh D. Duncan, Communication and the Social Order.
     New York: Bedminister Press, 1962.

38. Hugh D. Duncan, Symbols in Society. New York: Oxford
     University Press, 1968.

39. Karl A. Elling, Introduction to Modern Marketing: an
     Applied Approach. New York: Macmillan, 1969.

40. John W. Evans, "Evaluating Social Action Programs,"
     Social Science Quarterly. 50:568-81 (December 1969).

41. Edward Everett and George Ticknor, "On Libraries as
     Adult Education Institutions," in C. Hartley Grattan ed.,
     American Ideas About Adult Education, 1710-1951. New
     York: Bureau of Publications, Teachers College, Columbia
     University, 1959.

42. Merrill M. Flood, "Systems Analysis of Library
     Planning," Library Quarterly. 34:326-38 (October 1964).

43. Hardy Franklin, "Reaching the Non-User," Wilson
     Library Bulletin. 41:943-5 (May 1967).

44. John C. Frantz, "Big City Libraries: Strategy and
     Tactics for Change," Library Journal. 93:1968-70
     (May 15, 1968).

45. Erwin J. Gaines, "Urban Library Dilemma," Library
     Journal. 94:3966-70 (November 1, 1969).

46. Oliver Garceau, The Public Library in the Political
     Process. New York: Columbia University Press,
     1949.

47. John Gardner, Self-Renewal: the Individual and the
     Innovative Society. New York: Harper, 1963.

48. Guy Garrison, "Library Education and the Public
     Library," Library Journal. 95:2763-67 (September 1,
     1970).

49. Charles Y. Glock, Survey Research in the Social
     Sciences. New York: Russell Sage, 1967.

50.   J. E. Goldman, "Towards a National Technology
      Policy," Science. 177:1078-80 (September 22, 1972).

51.   W. Gove, "Organizing the Poor: an Evaluation of a
      Strategy," Social Science Quarterly. 50:673-756
      (December 1969).

52.   C. Hartley Grattan, In Quest of Knowledge. New York:
      Association Press, 1955.

53.   Emerson Greenaway, "Social Responsibility of Libraries,"
      PLA Bulletin. 25:12- 18 (January 1970).

54.   Edward T. Hall, The Silent Language. Garden City,
      N. Y.: Doubleday, 1959.

55.   Jill Hamberg, Where It's At. Boston: New England
      Free Press, 1967.

56.   Robert P. Hars, "Floating Academic Librarian,"
      American Libraries. 2:1169-73 (December 1971).

57.   Robert Havighurst, Human Development and Education.
      New York: Longmans Green, 1953.

58.   Hottest Spot in Town. 16mm., color, 39 minute.
      Missouri State Library and Missouri Library
      Association, 1968.

59.   Cyril O. Houle, "Responsibility of Library Trustees
      for Adult Education" A. L. A. Bulletin. November 1946.

60.   J. A. Howard, "Buyer Behavior and Related Technological
      Advances," Journal of Marketing Research. 34:18-21
      (January 1970).

61.   John Huenefeld, Community Activitists Handbook.
      Boston: Beacon Press, 1970.

62.   Raymond C. Hummel, Urban Education in America.
      New York: Oxford University Press, 1973.

63.   Floyd G. Hunter, Community Power Structure.
      Chapel Hill: University of North Carolina Press, 1953.

64. Information Volunteer Services, Directory of Agencies.
     Pittsburgh: Allegheny County Health and Welfare, 1971.

65. Phillip E. Jacob, Values and their Function in Decision
     Making. Philadelphia: University of Pennsylvania Studies
     of Social Values and Public Policy, 1962.

66. Alvin Johnson, The Public Library: a People's Univer-
     sity. New York: American Association for Adult Ed-
     ucation, 1938.

67. Alfred Kahn, Neighborhood Information Centers. New
     York: Columbia University Press, 1966.

68. Elihu Katz, Personal Influence. Glencoe, Ill.: Free
     Press, 1955.

69. Homer Kempfer, Identifying Educational Needs of Adults.
     (Circular No. 330, Federal Security Agency, Office of
     Education). Washington, D.C.: U.S. Government Printing
     Office, 1951.

70. Joseph T. Klapper, Effects of Mass Communication.
     New York: Free Press, 1960.

71. Malcolm S. Knowles, Adult Education Movement in the
     United States. New York: Holt, Rinehart and Winston,
     1962.

72. Dan Lacy, Freedom and Communication. 2nd ed.
     Urbana: University of Illinois Press, 1965.

73. Wilfrid Lancaster, ed., "Systems Design and Analysis
     for Libraries," Library Trends. 21:463-603, (April 1973).

74. William S. Learned, American Public Library and the
     Diffusion of Knowledge. New York: Harcourt, 1924.

75. Robert E. Lee, "Adult Education" in Encyclopedia of
     Library and Information Science. Vol. 1. New York:
     Marcel Dekker, 1968-

76. Robert Lee, Continuing Education for Adults Through
     the American Public Library. Chicago: American
     Library Association, 1966.

77.   Jean Legg, "Coordinating Library Services Within the
      Community," American Libraries. 1:457-63 (May 1970).

78.   Robert Leigh, Public Library in the United States. New
      York: Columbia University Press, 1950.

79.   "Library Rights for Adults: a Call for Action," ASD
      Newsletter. 7:2-3 (Fall 1970).

80.   "Library Services: a Bill of Rights for Adults," Library
      Journal. 94:2745-6 (August 1969).

81.   Library Social Action Institute, Library Social Action:
      Selective Reading List. Madison: Library School,
      University of Wisconsin, 1972.

82.   Marjorie Lincoln, "Pyramid Theory for Winning Library
      Elections," Illinois Libraries. 52:462-69 (May 1970).

83.   Edward C. Lindeman, The Community. New York:
      Association Press, 1921.

84.   Ronald Lippitt, Dynamics of Planned Change. New
      York: Harcourt, Brace and World, 1958.

85.   David J. Luck, Marketing Research. 3rd ed. Englewood
      Cliffs, N. J.: Prentice-Hall, 1970.

86.   F. J. Lyden, "Citizen Participation in Policy Making,"
      Social Science Quarterly. 50:631-42 (December 1969).

87.   Helen H. Lyman, ed., "Library Programs and Services
      to the Disadvantaged," Library Trends. 20:187-471
      (October 1971.

88.   Ellen McCardle, Nonverbal Communication. New York:
      Marcel Dekker, 1974.

89.   Lucy Maddox, Trends and Issues in American Library
      Association, 1876-1885. Ph.D. Thesis, University of
      Michigan, 1958.

90.   Allie Beth Martin, "The Librarian as Politician: an
      Essential Responsibility," New Mexico Libraries. 3:40-3
      (Summer 1970).

91.   Lowell A. Martin, Library Response to Urban Change:
      a Study of the Chicago Public Library. Chicago: American
      Library Association, 1969.

92.   H. Curtis Mial, "Community Development," Library
      Journal. 2195-2200 (October 15, 1955).

93.   William R. Monat, The Public Library and Its Com-
      munity. University Park, Pennsylvania: Pennsylvania
      State University, 1967.

94.   Judith Mowery, "Don't Just Stand There: the Librarian
      as Activist," Ohio Library Association Bulletin. 40:
      18-20 (January 1970).

95.   National Federation of Settlements and Neighborhood
      Centers, Local Community Structure and Civic Partic-
      ipation. Clearinghouse, U. S. Department of Commerce,
      Springfield, Virginia, 1968.

96.   New York Civil Liberties Union, The Burden of Blame:
      a Report on the Ocean Hill-Brownsville School Contro-
      versy. October 9, 1968.

97.   New York Librarian's Round Table on the Social Respon-
      sibilities of Libraries, Social Responsibilities of Libraries:
      The New York City Round Table Experience. Reproduced
      from typescript by the R. R. Bowkder Company for dis-
      tribution at the ALA Midwinter Meeting, 1969.

98.   E. B. Nyquist, "Poverty, Prejudice and the Public
      Library," Library Quarterly. 38:78-89 (January 1968).

99.   Martin Oppenheimer, Manual for Direct Action. Chicago:
      Quadrangle Books, 1964.

100. Talcott Parsons, Structure of Social Action. New York:
      McGraw-Hill, 1937.

101.   Patrick R. Penland, Communication Science and
       Technology. New York: Marcel Dekker, 1974.

102.   Patrick R. Penland, "Communication Versus Infor-
       mation," Proceedings, American Society for Infor-
       mation Science, Vol. 6, 1969. Westport, Connecticut:
       Greenwood Publishing, 1969.

103.   Patrick R. Penland, "Community and the Library,"
       Encyclopedia of Library and Information Science.
       New York: Marcel Dekker, 1968-

104.   Patrick R. Penland and James G. Williams, Community
       Psychology and Coordination. New York: Marcel Dekker,
       1974.

105.   Patrick R. Penland and James G. Williams, "Cybernetic
       Analysis of Communication Systems," Proceedings, In-
       ternational Conference on Information Science, Tel Aviv,
       Israel: August 29-September 3, 1971.

106.   Patrick R. Penland, "Educational Media and Technology,"
       Encyclopedia of Library and Information Science. New
       York: Marcel Dekker, 1968-

107.   Patrick R. Penland, "Floating Librarians," Encyclopedia
       of Library and Information Science. New York: Marcel
       Dekker, 1968-

108.   Patrick R. Penland, Floating Librarians in the Community.
       Bookstore, University of Pittsburgh, 1970.

109.   Patrick R. Penland and Sara Fine, Group Dynamics and
       Personnel Development. New York: Marcel Dekker,
       1974.

110.   Patrick R. Penland, "Helping the Public Librarian to
       Work as an Adult Educator," Adult Leadership. 9:
       298-300 (April 1961).

111.   Patrick R. Penland and Aleyamma Mathai, Interpersonal
       Communication. New York: Marcel Dekker, 1974.

112.   Patrick R. Penland et al, Manual for the Library-
        Community Encounter Simulation. Graduate School
        of Library and Information Science, University of
        Pittsburgh, 1970.

113.   Eleanor Phinney, Library Adult Education in Action.
        Chicago: American Library Association, 1956.

114.   Eleanor Phinney, "Library Adult Services and the War
        on Poverty," Illinois Libraries. 48:533-39 (September
        1966).

115.   Richard W. Poston, Democracy is You. New York:
        Harper, 1953.

116.   John W. Powell, Education for Maturity. New York:
        Heritage House, 1949.

117.   John W. Powell, Learning Comes of Age. New York:
        Association Press, 1956.

118.   Ruth E. Raines, Friends of the Library as Public
        Relations. Thesis, Southern Connecticut State College,
        1964.

119.   V. G. Rosenblum, "Controlling the Bureaucracy of
        the Antipoverty Program," Law and Contemporary
        Problems. 31:187-210 (Winter 1966).

120.   Arnold P. Sable, "Whither Public Service in America?"
        Wilson Library Bulletin. 45:390-3 (December 1970).

121.   Irwin T. Sanders, Making Good Communities Better.
        rev. ed., Lexington: University of Kentucky Press, 1967.

122.   Clarence A. Schoenfeld, Publicity Media and Methods.
        New York: Macmillan, 1963.

123.   Pat Schuman, "Commitment, Action and the 16th Street
        Manifesto," Ohio Library Association Bulletin. 40:4-9
        (January 1970).

124. D. A. Schwartz, "Measuring the Effectiveness of Your Company's Advertising," Journal of Marketing. 33:20-5 (April 1969).

125. John B. Shaw, "Role of the Layman in the Library and the Relations Between the Professional and the Layman," Oklahoma Librarian. October 1966.

126. Carolyn W. Sherif, Attitude and Attitude Change: The Social Judgment-Involvement Approach. Philadelphia: Saunders, 1965.

127. Muzafer Sherif, In Common Predicament: Social Psychology of Intergroup Conflict and Cooperation. Boston: Houghton-Mifflin, 1966.

128. Muzafer Sherif and Carl I. Hovland, Social Judgment. New Haven, Conn.: Yale University Press, 1961.

129. Charles D. Spielberger, ed., Current Topics in Clinical and Community Psychology. Vol. 3, New York: Academic Press, 1971.

130. Charles S. Steinberg, The Mass Communicators: Public Relations, Public Opinion and Mass Media. New York: Harper, 1958.

131. Grace T. Stevenson, "We Strive for Excellence," Minnesota Libraries. 20:91-6 (December 1961).

132. Carla J. Stoffle, "Public Library Service to the Disadvantage: a Comprehensive Annotated Bibliography, 1964-68," Library Journal. 94:141-52 (January 15, 1969); 94:507-15 (February 1, 1969).

133. C. Walter Stone, "Adult Education and the Public Library," Library Trends. 1:437-453 (April 1953).

134. C. Walter Stone, Library Program for Columbia. Washington, D. C.: Council on Library Resources, 1965.

135. Lee Thayer, Communication: General Semantics Perspectives. New York: Spartan Books, 1970.

136.   Victor Thompson, Bureaucracy and Innovation. Bir-
        mingham: University of Alabama Press, 1969.

137.   William I. Thompson, "The Individual as Institution,"
        Harper's. 245:48-62 (September 1972).

138.   Allen Tough, Adults Learning Projects. Toronto:
        Ontario Institute for Studies in Education, 1971.

139.   Arnuflo D. Trejo, "Library Service for the Spanish
        Speaking," ALA Bulletin. 63:1077-81 (September 1969).

140.   Dorothy A. Turick, ed., "Neighborhood Information
        Center," RQ. 12:341-363 (Summer, 1973).

141.   John B. Turner, ed., Neighborhood Organization
        for Community Action. New York: National Association
        of Social Workers, 1968.

142.   U. S. Department of the Interior, Bureau of Education,
        Public Libraries in the United States of America, Their
        History, Condition and Management. Washington, D.C.:
        U. S. Government Printing Office, 1876.

143.   Coolie Verner, Adult Education: Theory and Method.
        Chicago: Adult Education Association, 1962.

144.   Douglas Waples, What Reading Does to People. Chicago:
        University of Chicago Press, 1940.

145.   Roland L. Warren, Studying Your Community. New
        York: Free Press, 1965.

146.   Roland L. Warren, Types of Purposive Social Change
        at the Community Level. University Papers in Social
        Welfare, No. 11, Waltham, Mass.: Brandeis Univer-
        sity, 1965.

147.   Katherine Weibel, "The Floating Librarian," in
        Patrick R. Penland, Floating Librarians in the
        Community. Bookstore, University of Pittsburgh,
        1970.

148. Ulf Wennerberg, "Using the Delphi Technique for
      Planning the Future of Libraries," Unesco Bulletin
      for Libraries. 26:242-26 (September 1972).

149. Joseph Wheeler, Library and the Community. Chicago:
      American Library Association, 1924.

150. B. Whitaker, "Strengthening the Ombudsman," New
      Statesman. 79:179-80 (Feb. 6, 1970).

151. James G. Williams, Simulation and Games. New York:
      Marcel Dekker, 1974.

152. M. C. Yovits, "Generalized Theory for the Effectiveness
      and Utilization of Information," Proceedings, International
      Conference on Information Science, Tel Aviv, Israel, 1971.

INDEX